Donor-Centric Fundraising

I0409564

By Art Fuller, PhD

Building Lasting Relationships

INTRODUCTION

Amazon has a leadership principle which serves as the foundation of their business. It is called Customer Obsession. The idea behind customer obsession is that the company looks at what's best for the customer and works backward from there. This is where great ideas like free shipping, two day shipping, drones that provide order-fulfillment in a little as one hour originated. Amazon determined that getting an order fulfilled faster than you could drive to a physical store was what was best for the customer. It's also why their product return process is so simple. You can literally say, "I don't what his item anymore" and they will refund your money. No hassle. No arguing. Return it to any number of locations like the UPS store or Kohl's and you're done with it. You don't need to re-wrap it or even have the original packaging. Just drop it off. They take care of the rest...

Why would Amazon, a trillion dollar company fuss so much over its customers? Because without them they wouldn't have a business. Likewise, non-profits could be very successful it they adopted a donor-centric mindset. Donors, like Amazon's retail customers, are the lifeblood of any non-profit. What do *they* think about your amazing, new idea? Are you making it as easy as possible for *them* to commit and give to your organization? Is your communication with them in a manner and method of *their* preference or what's easiest for you?

This book will endeavor to refocus your thinking about donors if you haven't been donor-obsessed in the past. If you have been donor-obsessed, this work will provide you with new insights into how you can further increase your focus on donors. NOTE: I will use the term donor-centric and donor-focused synonymously throughout this work.

While I certainly encourage reading the book from start to finish, more than that this tome is a reference book of strategies, best practices, suggestions and helps for specific questions and situations. Got a question about how to conduct donor research? Check out Chapter 2. Need to improve your donor acquisition and retention? Check out the techniques listed in Chapter 4... ETC.

Happy reading and happy fundraising,

Art Fuller, PhD - August 2023

TABLE OF CONTENTS

Dedication

Regardless of your experience, station in life, job prospects for the future, etc., nobody succeeds alone. We all have someone or many someones who showed us the ropes of the job; taught us what to do and when to do it.

For me, in the brand-new world of fundraising that person was my good friend, Wes Powell. Wes has been helping non-profits raise money literally for decades. I remember my first day on the job in this new arena. Training consisted of 'listening in' on phone calls that Wes made to clients.

After 45 minutes of this 'eaves-dropping', I was convinced I could not do this type of work. Clients had too many questions to which *I knew* I did not have a clue about the answer. Yet, here was Wes... effortlessly answering their queries and suggesting various strategies for them to implement. He made it look easy!

I stayed with the job (because I had moved to Atlanta to work) and over the next few months gradually acquired some of that confidence that Wes exuded. There were still many phone calls where I put a client on hold after telling them, 'Let me place you on hold for just a minute. I need to get a resource...' That resource was Wes.

Art Fuller, PhD   6

"Wes, help! I've got a client that is asking how do they do A, B, C... What should I tell them?"

Wes would casually explain, 'Tell them to do C, D and E. Then check back with us in 30 days."

I would return to the call, offer the recommendation and conclude with another satisfied customer.

So, Wes hats off to you for all your help, sharing of your expertise and just general support especially during those early days in this new world of fundraising and stewardship!

I happily dedicate this book to you!

Art Fuller, PhD
August 2023

Chapter 1 - Introduction to Donor-Centric Fundraising

- Understanding the importance of donor-centric fundraising
- Exploring the benefits of building lasting relationships with donors
- Identifying key principles and best practices in donor-focused fundraising

Understanding the Importance of Donor-Centric Fundraising

In the world of nonprofit organizations, fundraising is a vital component of sustainability and impact. Traditionally, fundraising strategies have focused primarily on the organization's needs and goals. However, a paradigm shift has occurred in recent years, placing greater emphasis on donor-centric fundraising. Donor-centric fundraising is an approach that prioritizes understanding and meeting the needs of donors, creating meaningful relationships, and fostering long-term engagement. In this chapter, we will explore the importance of donor-centric fundraising and its impact on nonprofit organizations.

Here are some of the primary benefits of donor-centric fundraising:

It Builds Strong Relationships: Donor-centric fundraising recognizes that donors are not just sources of financial support but also valuable partners in advancing the organization's mission. By shifting the focus from transactions to relationships, nonprofits can build strong connections with their donors. This approach involves understanding donors' motivations, interests, and values, and aligning fundraising efforts to resonate with them. By fostering meaningful relationships, nonprofits can create a loyal and engaged donor base that is more likely to provide ongoing support.

It Enhances Donor Satisfaction: When donors feel valued and appreciated, they are more likely to continue their support and even increase their contributions over time. Donor-centric fundraising strategies prioritize donor satisfaction by personalizing communication, expressing gratitude, and providing opportunities for engagement. By actively listening to donors, addressing their concerns, and recognizing their impact, nonprofits can cultivate a positive donor experience that fosters long-term loyalty.

It Maximizes Fundraising Results: Donor-centric fundraising is not just about making donors feel good; it also yields tangible benefits for nonprofit organizations. When fundraising efforts align with donors' interests and motivations, they are more likely to respond positively and contribute more generously. By tailoring fundraising appeals, events, and campaigns to the specific *needs and preferences of donors*, nonprofits can optimize their fundraising results and achieve greater financial sustainability.

It Increases Donor Retention: Donor retention is a critical factor in the success of any fundraising program. Donor-centric fundraising recognizes that retaining existing donors is more cost-effective than acquiring new ones. By focusing on building relationships, providing personalized experiences, and demonstrating the impact of donations, nonprofits can increase donor retention rates. This not only ensures a stable base of support but also reduces the need for constant donor acquisition efforts.

 **Personal Timeout (PT)** - We'll be taking these from time to time. I'll use them to share a bit of real world experience or wisdom. In this instance,

I worked previously for one of the largest battery manufacturers in the world. Their Customer Service department had a saying that it was easier (and cheaper) to keep the customers they had happy than to continually replace them with new ones. In the church world, it can generally take one to two years to grow a donor / tither to where they are giving regular, significant support. I've worked with organizations that seem to think donors grew on trees. They experienced such rapid growth in their attendance / giving base, they thought it would never end, regardless of how they treated supporters. Some of them hit a financial brick wall as attendance growth slowed and giving growth / dollars was right behind it. Staff reductions and layoffs weren't long after...

Long story short - Take care of the donors you currently have as well as trying to accumulate new ones along the way.

It Drives Donor Acquisition: While retaining existing donors is crucial, donor-centric fundraising also plays a role in acquiring new supporters. Satisfied and engaged donors are more likely to become advocates for the organization, spreading the word and attracting others to get involved. By prioritizing the needs and interests of donors, nonprofits can leverage their existing donor base to expand their reach and acquire new supporters through positive word-of-mouth and referrals.

It Encourages Major Gifts and Legacy Giving: Donor-centric fundraising can pave the way for major gifts and legacy giving. When donors feel a strong connection to the organization and believe in its mission, they may be more inclined to make significant contributions or include the organization in their estate plans. By cultivating deep relationships and demonstrating the impact of donations, nonprofits can inspire donors to make transformative gifts that can significantly impact the organization's long-term sustainability.

It Nurtures Community and Trust: Donor-centric fundraising creates a sense of community and trust between the nonprofit organization and its supporters. When donors feel valued and involved, they are more likely to become advocates for the organization's cause. They become part of a community of like-minded individuals who share a common vision. This sense of belonging fosters trust, transparency, and accountability, further strengthening the bond between the organization and its donors.

In conclusion, donor-centric fundraising is a powerful approach that prioritizes understanding and meeting the needs of donors. By building strong relationships, enhancing donor satisfaction, maximizing fundraising results, increasing donor retention, driving donor acquisition, encouraging major gifts and legacy giving, nurturing community and trust.

***

Exploring the benefits of building lasting relationships with donors

For nonprofit organizations, building lasting relationships with donors is a fundamental aspect of sustainable fundraising and long-term success. While acquiring new donors is important, nurturing and maintaining relationships with existing donors can yield significant benefits (one at least is in the lower cost to solicit their giving). In this section, we will explore the various advantages of building lasting relationships with donors and how they contribute to the overall growth and impact of nonprofit organizations.

BENEFIT #1 - Increased Donor Loyalty. Building lasting relationships fosters a sense of loyalty among donors. When donors feel connected to an organization and its mission, they are more likely to remain engaged and committed over time. By consistently demonstrating the impact of their contributions and recognizing their support, nonprofits can create a loyal donor base that provides ongoing financial support and advocacy. Donors who feel appreciated and valued are less likely to shift their philanthropic focus elsewhere, resulting in increased donor retention rates.

BENEFIT #2 - Enhanced Trust and Credibility. Building lasting relationships with donors is a powerful way to establish trust and credibility. When nonprofits consistently deliver on their promises, communicate transparently, and demonstrate effective stewardship of resources, donors develop confidence in the organization's ability to create meaningful change. Trust is an essential element in philanthropy, and donors are ~~more likely~~ **WILL** support organizations they trust. By prioritizing lasting relationships, nonprofits can build a solid reputation and attract new donors based on the trust they have earned from their existing supporters.

BENEFIT #3 - Increased Donor Engagement. Lasting relationships with donors leads to increased engagement. Donors who feel connected to an organization are more likely to actively participate in its activities, events, and initiatives. They may volunteer their time, serve on advisory boards, or contribute their skills and expertise. Engaged donors become ambassadors for the organization, spreading awareness of its mission and inspiring others to get involved. By fostering lasting relationships, nonprofits can tap into the passion and commitment of their donors, creating a vibrant and active community of supporters.

BENEFIT #4 - Higher Lifetime Donor Value. Building lasting relationships with donors can significantly impact their lifetime value. When donors are engaged and loyal, they are more likely to increase the frequency and size of their contributions over time. By cultivating relationships and demonstrating the impact of donations, nonprofits can encourage donors to become major gift donors or include the organization in their estate plans. The cumulative effect of long-term relationships is higher lifetime donor value, which can have a transformative impact on the organization's financial sustainability and capacity to fulfill its mission.

BENEFIT #5 - Improved Donor Insights. Lasting relationships provide nonprofits with valuable insights into their donors. By understanding donors' motivations, interests, and preferences, nonprofits can tailor their fundraising strategies and communication efforts more effectively. Through ongoing engagement and feedback, nonprofits can gather data and feedback that inform programming decisions and shape the organization's future direction. The deep understanding gained through lasting relationships allows nonprofits to make informed decisions that resonate with their donors and drive long-term impact.

BENEFIT #6 - Opportunities for Collaboration. Lasting relationships create opportunities for collaboration between nonprofits and their donors. Donors who are deeply connected to an organization's mission may bring additional resources, expertise, or networks to the table. Collaboration can take various forms, including joint initiatives, co-funding opportunities, or strategic partnerships. By nurturing lasting relationships, nonprofits can tap into the diverse skills and resources of their donors, enhancing their capacity to achieve their goals.

BENEFIT #7 - Positive Word-of-Mouth and Referrals. Satisfied and engaged donors are likely to become advocates for the organization. By building lasting relationships, nonprofits can turn donors into ambassadors who share their positive experiences and actively promote the organization's work. These advocates can spread awareness, attract new donors, and expand the organization's network. Positive word-of-mouth and referrals from existing donors carry significant weight and can contribute to the growth and sustainability of the nonprofit.

In summary, building lasting relationships will contribute to the overall growth and impact of your nonprofit organization.

***

Identifying key principles and best practices in donor-focused fundraising

Donor-focused fundraising is an approach that prioritizes understanding and meeting the needs of donors to build meaningful relationships and achieve sustainable fundraising results. To effectively implement this approach, nonprofit organizations must adhere to key principles and adopt best practices that guide their fundraising strategies. In this section, we will explore the three essential principles and associated best practices in donor-focused fundraising that can lead to success and long-term sustainability.

Principle #1: Donor-Centricity

Donor-centricity is at the core of donor-focused fundraising. It involves recognizing that donors are not merely sources of financial support but individuals with their own motivations, interests, and values. Adopting a donor-centric approach means putting the needs and preferences of donors at the forefront of fundraising efforts. This principle emphasizes personalization, effective communication, and building relationships based on mutual understanding and respect.

Best Practices:

a. *Conduct donor research:* Gather data and insights about your donors through surveys, interviews, and analytics to understand their demographics, giving history, motivations, and communication preferences.

b. *Develop donor personas:* Create fictional representations of your ideal donors based on the research and data collected. Use these personas to guide your fundraising strategies and tailor your communications to resonate with each persona.

c. *Segment your donor base:* Group donors with similar characteristics or giving patterns together to create targeted approaches that address their specific interests and needs.

d. *Personalize donor communications:* Customize your messages and appeals to reflect the interests and motivations of individual donors. Use their preferred communication channels and language that resonates with them.

Principle #2: Relationship Building

Building strong and meaningful relationships with donors is essential for successful donor-focused fundraising. Relationship building involves cultivating connections, demonstrating appreciation, and engaging donors in a way that fosters trust, loyalty, and long-term commitment. It requires ongoing communication, transparency, and active stewardship of the donor relationship.

Best Practices:
a. *Express gratitude:* Regularly acknowledge and thank donors for their contributions, ensuring they feel appreciated and valued.

b. *Provide regular updates:* Keep donors informed about the impact of their donations and the progress of your organization's programs and initiatives. Share success stories, outcomes, and milestones to demonstrate the value of their support.

c. *Foster two-way communication:* Encourage dialogue with donors, listening to their feedback, suggestions, and concerns. Respond promptly and transparently, showing that their opinions matter and are taken into account.

d. *Engage donors beyond fundraising:* Offer opportunities for donors to get involved beyond monetary contributions. Invite them to events, volunteer activities, or join advisory boards to foster a sense of community and shared ownership in the organization's mission.

Principle #3 Donor Stewardship

Donor stewardship focuses on nurturing and strengthening the donor relationship over time. It involves proactive and strategic efforts to engage, retain, and upgrade donors. Donor stewardship goes beyond transactional interactions, aiming to provide a personalized and exceptional experience for donors.

Best Practices:

a. Develop a stewardship plan: Create a comprehensive plan that outlines the touchpoints, activities, and communications designed to steward donors throughout their relationship with the organization.

b. Provide regular and meaningful communication: Keep donors informed about the impact of their contributions, how their support is making a difference, and the organization's future plans. Customize communication based on donor preferences and interests.

c. Recognize and acknowledge donor support: Publicly recognize donors through donor walls, annual reports, or social media platforms. Tailor recognition efforts to match donor preferences, whether it's public acknowledgment or more discreet forms of recognition.

d. *Offer exclusive benefits and opportunities:* Provide special benefits, invitations, or access to exclusive events or experiences for donors. This helps foster a sense of belonging and deepens the donor's connection to the organization.

Chapter 2 - Knowing Your Donors

- **Conducting comprehensive donor research and segmentation**
- **Utilizing data analysis to understand donor behavior and preferences**
- **Developing donor personas to inform fundraising strategies**

Welcome to chapter 2 of the donor-focused fundraising approach, "Knowing Your Donors." In chapter 1, we discussed the importance of donor-centric fundraising and how it can transform your organization's fundraising efforts. Now, in chapter 2, we will dive deeper into understanding the unique individuals who make up *YOUR* donor base. By gaining insights into their motivations, preferences, and behavior, you will be equipped to tailor your fundraising strategies effectively and build strong, lasting relationships.

In this chapter, we will explore the various methods and techniques that will help you gain a comprehensive understanding of your donors. By examining their demographics, motivations, communication preferences, and giving patterns, you will uncover valuable insights that will inform your fundraising strategies and maximize your impact. We will guide you through the process of understanding your donors, from conducting research to developing personas and leveraging data.

By gaining insights into their motivations, preferences, and behavior, you can develop strategies that resonate with them on a personal level, build strong relationships, and maximize your fundraising impact.

By the end of this chapter, you will have the knowledge and tools necessary to conduct effective donor research, develop donor personas, segment your donor base, and leverage data and analytics to inform your fundraising strategies. You will gain insights that will enable you to cultivate strong relationships with your donors and create customized experiences that resonate with their unique preferences and motivations. So, let's dive in and discover the power of knowing your donors!

Conducting Comprehensive Donor Research and Segmentation

Knowing your donors is the foundation of successful donor-centric fundraising. To effectively engage with donors and create personalized fundraising strategies, nonprofit organizations must conduct comprehensive donor research and segmentation. By gathering data and insights about donors, organizations can better understand their preferences, motivations, and giving patterns. This knowledge allows nonprofits to tailor their communication, cultivation, and solicitation efforts, ultimately maximizing donor engagement and fundraising outcomes. In this chapter, we will explore the key steps involved in conducting comprehensive donor research and segmentation.

How To Conduct Donor Research -

Key Step 1. Define Your Research Objectives:

Before embarking on donor research, it is essential to define clear objectives. What specific information do you seek to gather? Are you looking to understand donor demographics, motivations, communication preferences, or giving history? Defining your research objectives will guide the research process and ensure that the data collected aligns with your organization's needs.

Key Step 2. Choose Your Research Methods:

Donor research can be conducted through various methods, including surveys, interviews, focus groups, and data analysis. Each method offers unique advantages and insights. Surveys allow for quantitative data collection, while interviews and focus groups offer qualitative insights through direct conversations with donors. Combining multiple methods can provide a comprehensive view of your donor base.

Key Step 3. Deep Dive into Demographic Analysis:

One crucial aspect of donor research is demographic analysis. Demographic information such as age, gender, location, and occupation can provide valuable insights into donor characteristics and preferences. Analyzing this data helps identify trends and patterns within your donor base and enables you to tailor your fundraising strategies accordingly.

Key Step 4. Motivation Assessment:

Understanding donor motivations is key to building strong relationships. It is essential to explore why donors support your organization, what aspects of your mission resonate with them, and how they wish to make an impact. Surveys, interviews, and focus groups can be effective tools to assess donor motivations, allowing you to align your messaging and fundraising appeals with their interests and values.

Key Step 5. Communication Preferences:
Learning how donors prefer to be communicated with is vital for effective engagement. Some donors may prefer email updates, while others may appreciate texts, phone calls or personalized letters. By gathering information on communication preferences, you can tailor your outreach and engagement efforts to match donor expectations, ensuring that your messages reach and resonate with them effectively.

Key Step 6. Giving History and Patterns:
Analyzing donor giving history provides insights into their level of engagement and commitment. Examining the frequency, timing, and size of donations can help identify patterns and trends. Are there specific times of the year when donors are more likely to contribute? Are there consistent donors who could be potential major gift prospects? By segmenting donors based on their giving history, you can tailor your stewardship and solicitation strategies to their unique preferences.

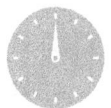

Personal Timeout (PT) - I have been

Art Fuller, PhD   26

privileged to personally analyze the giving data of over 2,500 non-profit clients. There are definite patterns and profiles that re-appear over and over based on the size of the donor base, type of non-profit and even geographic location of the majority of donors... In terms of churches, I have identified at least four organizational stewardship profiles that have specific characteristics with specific prescriptives for increasing donor engagement. This financial analysis approach, which seems very common and natural now, was pioneered by Dave Sutherland, former CEO of INJOY Stewardship Solutions. Dave developed his initial analysis organically by responding to the need to demonstrate and convince a client they had a successful fundraising campaign. I worked alongside Dave, incorporating his feedback and suggestions, refining this approach until it became a distinctive of the organization. It has been adopted by most fundraising organizations today.

Key Step 7. Data Management and Analysis:
Effectively managing donor data is crucial for successful research and segmentation. Utilize a robust donor management system or customer relationship management (CRM) software to collect, store, and analyze donor information securely. Conduct regular data cleaning and validation processes to ensure accuracy. Inaccurate data is worse than having no data.

Data analysis techniques such as clustering and predictive modeling can further enhance your understanding of donor behavior and preferences.

Key Step 8. Segmentation Strategies:
Once you have collected donor data, the next step is to segment your donor base. Segmentation involves grouping donors with similar characteristics or giving patterns to create targeted approaches. Common segmentation criteria include demographics, giving capacity, giving frequency, and engagement levels. By segmenting your donors, you can develop tailored communication and solicitation strategies that resonate with each group, resulting in more effective fundraising outcomes.

Key Step 9. Ongoing Monitoring and Evaluation:
Donor research and segmentation should be an ongoing process. Donor preferences and behaviors may change over time, and it is essential to stay updated. Continuously monitor and evaluate the effectiveness of your segmentation strategies, and make adjustments as necessary. Regularly solicit donor feedback and conduct surveys to gather insights on their evolving preferences.

***

Utilizing data analysis to understand donor
behavior and preferences

In the age of technology and information, nonprofits have access to vast amounts of donor data that can provide valuable insights into their behavior and preferences. However, data alone is not enough. It is crucial to effectively analyze and interpret that data to gain meaningful insights that inform fundraising strategies. By utilizing data analysis techniques, nonprofits can understand donor behavior, identify trends, and tailor their approaches to maximize donor engagement and fundraising success. In this section, we will explore how data analysis can help nonprofits understand donor behavior and preferences.

DAT (Data Analysis Technique) **1. Collect Relevant Data**:
The first step in utilizing data analysis is to collect relevant and accurate donor data. This data can come from various sources, including donor databases, fundraising platforms, surveys, and website analytics. Key data points to collect include demographics, giving history, communication preferences, event attendance, and online engagement. Be sure your data collection processes comply with privacy regulations and ethical standards.

DAT 2. Cleaning and Preparing Data:

Before conducting data analysis, it is essential to clean and prepare the data. This involves removing duplicates, correcting errors, standardizing formats, and ensuring data consistency. Clean data ensures accurate analysis and prevents misleading insights. Consider using data management software or customer relationship management (CRM) systems to facilitate this process.

Personal Timeout (PT) - It's critical you qualify the data for accuracy before starting to analyze it. This sounds simplistic but *don't assume any data you collect or are sent is correct*. Review it, study it, verify it. Call the client and ask a few questions. Is my understanding correct here - this actually equals that, etc.? Does it make sense? Is it reasonable knowing other factors I know about this client?

A consulting coworker of mine received some financial data from a client, analyzed it and went onsite to present their analysis. They had failed to ask any qualifying questions on the front end about the information which turned out to be incomplete and incorrect. Needless to say the resulting analysis was totally wrong and the coworker totally embarrassed as the client asked question after question about erroneous conclusions based on faulty data. Failure to qualify the data prior to analysis ended up in the consultant being removed from working with this client. The customer had lost all confidence in their expertise all because they had failed to verify the data.

DAT 3. Segmentation and Clustering:
Segmentation is the process of grouping donors based on shared characteristics or behaviors. By segmenting donors, nonprofits can tailor their communication and solicitation strategies to specific groups, maximizing engagement and response rates. Clustering analysis techniques can identify patterns within the data, allowing for more precise segmentation. Common segmentation criteria include demographics, giving history, and engagement levels.

DAT 4. RFM Analysis:
Recency, Frequency, Monetary (RFM) analysis is a powerful technique for understanding donor behavior. It assesses the recency of donors' last contribution, the frequency of their donations, and the monetary value of their contributions. By categorizing donors into RFM segments, nonprofits can identify their most valuable donors, potential major gift prospects, and those who require re-engagement strategies.

DAT 5. Predictive Analytics:

Predictive analytics leverages historical donor data to make informed predictions about future behavior and preferences. By utilizing statistical models and machine learning algorithms, nonprofits can identify patterns and trends that predict donor actions. Predictive analytics can help identify potential major donors, forecast giving trends, and personalize solicitations based on individual donor propensities.

DAT 6. Data Visualization:

Data analysis results are most impactful when presented in a visually engaging format. Data visualization tools, such as charts, graphs, and dashboards, can help nonprofits interpret and communicate complex information effectively. Visual representations of donor behavior and preferences enable nonprofits to identify trends quickly, make informed decisions, and communicate insights to stakeholders.

DAT 7. A/B Testing:

A/B testing, also known as split testing, involves comparing two variations of a fundraising approach to determine which performs better. By randomly assigning donors to different groups and measuring their responses, nonprofits can test different strategies, messages, or communication channels. A/B testing allows organizations to optimize their fundraising efforts based on data-driven insights.

DAT 8. Donor Journey Mapping:
Donor journey mapping visualizes the stages and touch-points that donors go through from initial engagement to ongoing support. By analyzing donor data at each stage, nonprofits can identify opportunities for improvement, bottlenecks in the donor journey, and moments that drive increased engagement or attrition. Donor journey mapping helps organizations create more targeted and personalized experiences for donors.

DAT 9. Data-Driven Decision-Making:
Utilizing data analysis ultimately enables data-driven decision-making. Nonprofits can make informed choices about their fundraising strategies, communication channels, campaign targeting, and stewardship efforts. By relying on data rather than assumptions or guesswork, nonprofits can allocate resources more effectively, improve donor engagement, and leverage analytics to inform your fundraising strategies.

***

Developing donor personas to inform fundraising strategies

Why are Donor Personas Important?

The thesis of this work is that understanding your donors is key to building meaningful relationships and maximizing the success of your fundraising campaigns. One effective tool for gaining insights into your donor base is by developing donor personas. Donor personas are fictional representations of your ideal donors, based on real data and research. These personas provide a deeper understanding of donor motivations, preferences, and behavior, allowing you to tailor your fundraising strategies to resonate with your target audience. In this section, we will explore the importance of donor personas and discuss the process of developing them to inform your fundraising strategies.

Donor personas can play a crucial role in informing fundraising strategies for several reasons. Firstly, they help you humanize your donors. Instead of viewing them as faceless entities, personas allow you to create a relatable character, complete with demographics, motivations, and interests. This humanization facilitates a stronger emotional connection and a better understanding of your donors' needs.

Secondly, donor personas enable you to segment your donor base effectively. By grouping donors based on shared characteristics, you can develop targeted approaches that resonate with specific segments. For example, if you discover through persona development that a significant portion of your donors are passionate about environmental causes, you can design fundraising campaigns that emphasize the impact of their contributions on sustainability efforts.

Furthermore, personas guide your decision-making process. When you have a clear picture of your ideal donors, it becomes easier to prioritize fundraising activities and allocate resources accordingly. By focusing on the needs and preferences of your personas, you can optimize your efforts and achieve better results.

The Process of Developing Donor Personas

- **Gather Data:** The first step in developing donor personas is to collect relevant data about your donors. This can be done through surveys, interviews, website analytics, and donor databases. Look for patterns and commonalities among your donors in terms of age, location, giving history, communication preferences, and any other relevant information.

- Identify Key Characteristics: Analyze the data you have gathered to identify the most significant characteristics of your donors. These may include demographic information such as age, gender, income level, and occupation, as well as psychographic factors such as interests, values, and motivations. Group similar characteristics together to form distinct segments.

- Create Persona Profiles: Once you have identified the key characteristics, it's time to create persona profiles. Give each persona a name and provide a detailed description of their background, lifestyle, motivations, and preferences. Include information such as their philanthropic goals, preferred communication channels, and giving capacity. The more specific and detailed your personas are, the better you can align your fundraising strategies with their needs.

- Validate and Refine: It's essential to validate your personas by comparing them to real data and seeking feedback from your team and stakeholders. Refine the personas based on new insights and feedback, ensuring they accurately represent your donor base.

***

Applying Donor Personas to Fundraising Strategies

Once you have developed your donor personas, it's time to put them to work and inform your fundraising strategies. Here are four ways you can apply personas to maximize your fundraising efforts:

Application 1. Tailor Messaging and Storytelling: Craft your fundraising messages and storytelling to resonate with each persona. Use language, images, and narratives that align with their values, motivations, and interests. For example, if one of your personas is a young professional passionate about social justice, emphasize the impact of their contributions in creating a more equitable society.

Application 2. Choose the Right Channels: Based on your personas' preferred communication channels, select the appropriate platforms to reach out to them. If your persona is more active on social media, focus your efforts on platforms like Instagram or Twitter. If they prefer email communication, ensure your fundraising messages are emailed to them.

Application 3. Personalize Acknowledgments and Thank You Messages: Customize acknowledgment and thank you messages based on donor personas. Tailor these messages to reflect the specific impact and importance of each donor's contribution. Personalization shows appreciation and helps foster stronger relationships with donors.

Application 4. Develop Benefits and Recognition: Consider the preferences and preferences of each donor persona when designing donor recognition and benefits programs. Offer unique benefits that align with their interests, such as exclusive updates, access to events, or special recognition opportunities. This approach helps build loyalty and strengthens the donor-nonprofit relationship.

By applying donor personas to fundraising strategies, nonprofits can better understand and connect with their donors on a more personal level. This personalized approach will improve engagement, donor retention, and ultimately, fundraising success.

Chapter 3 - Crafting Compelling Donor Communications

- Creating donor-centered messaging and storytelling

- Creating a donor communication plan that encompasses various channels and touchpoints

- Designing effective fundraising appeals and campaigns
- Leveraging digital platforms for donor engagement and communication

Welcome to chapter 3 of donor-centric fundraising, "Crafting Compelling Donor Communications." In chapter 2, we explored the importance of knowing our donors and understanding their behavior and preferences. Now, in chapter 3, we will delve into the art of crafting effective and compelling communications that resonate with donors and inspire them to take action. Effective donor communications are key to building strong relationships, cultivating donor loyalty, and driving fundraising success.

Chapter Overview:

In this chapter, we will explore the essential elements of crafting compelling donor communications. We will discuss strategies to create messages that resonate with donors, techniques to engage and captivate their attention, and best practices for effective storytelling. We will also creat a donor communication plan that encompasses various channels and touchpoints

Throughout this chapter, we will provide practical tips and real-life examples to help you develop your donor communication skills. You will learn how to create messages that resonate with donors, captivate their attention, and inspire them to take action. By the end of this chapter, you will have the tools and knowledge necessary to craft compelling donor communications that strengthen relationships, drive engagement, and maximize fundraising success.

***

Creating donor-centered messaging and storytelling

In the world of fundraising, crafting donor-centered messaging and storytelling is crucial to engaging donors and inspiring them to support your cause. By tailoring your messages to the interests, values, and aspirations of your donors, you can create a deeper connection that motivates them to take action. In this section, we will explore the key elements of creating donor-centered messaging and storytelling that resonate with your donors and drive meaningful impact.

Element 1. Know Your Donors:
Before crafting any message, it is essential to have a deep understanding of your donors. Conduct thorough research and analysis to uncover their motivations, preferences, and values. What drives them to support your organization? What aspects of your mission resonate with them? Understanding your donors on a personal level enables you to create messaging that speaks directly to their interests and aspirations.

Element 2. Speak to Their Impact:
Donors want to know that *their* contributions make a difference. When crafting your

messaging, focus on the impact of *their* support. Show how *their* donations directly lead to positive outcomes and change lives. Use concrete examples, success stories, and data-driven evidence to demonstrate the difference their support makes. Highlight the beneficiaries of your work and emphasize how donors play a vital role in creating that impact.

Element 3. Use Donor-Centric Language:
To create donor-centered messaging, shift the focus from your organization to the donors themselves. Use language that acknowledges their importance and highlights their role as catalysts for change. Replace "we" and "our organization" with "you" and "your support." Make the donors feel like valued partners in your mission. By using donor-centric language, you make them the heroes of the story and create a stronger emotional connection.

Here's an **example of a donor-centric communication** to a new donor that has recently contributed to your organization -

Subject: Welcome to Our Community of Changemakers!

Dear [Donor's Name],

On behalf of [Non-Profit Organization's Name], I extend a warm and heartfelt welcome to our family of compassionate changemakers. Your recent contribution has made an immediate impact, and we are thrilled to have you on board as a valued partner in our mission to create positive change in [cause/issue area].

Your generous support enables us to drive transformative initiatives and bring hope to countless lives. We wanted to take a moment to share the incredible difference your contribution has already made:

[Highlight the Immediate Impact of the Donor's Contribution - e.g., "Thanks to your donation, ten underprivileged children received nutritious meals today, ensuring they no longer have to go to bed hungry."]

At [Non-Profit Organization's Name], we believe in putting donors like you at the heart of everything we do. Your commitment to [cause/issue area] empowers us to go above and beyond in our efforts to effect lasting change.

As a new member of our community, we are eager to keep you engaged and informed. In the coming weeks, you can expect:

- Personalized Updates: Regular communication sharing the progress of our programs and the impact of your support.
- Inspiring Stories: Heartwarming stories from the field, illustrating the lives you touch through your generosity.
- Exclusive Events: Invitations to participate in exclusive events that provide an inside look at

our organization's work and meet fellow supporters like yourself.

We are here to answer any questions you may have or provide further insights into our programs. Your thoughts and ideas matter to us, and we encourage you to share them with us at any time.

Once again, thank you for choosing to stand with us as a donor. Your belief in our mission strengthens our resolve to create a better world, together.

With gratitude and warm regards,

[Your Name]
[Your Title/Role]
[Non-Profit Organization's Name]
[Contact Information]

In this example, the communication is personalized, expresses gratitude, and highlights the immediate impact of the donor's contribution. It sets the stage for continued engagement by sharing upcoming benefits and outlining how the organization will keep the donor informed and involved in their efforts.

Element 4. Connect Emotionally:
Effective storytelling evokes emotions and connects with donors on a deeper level. Craft narratives that resonate with their values, experiences, and aspirations. Share compelling stories that showcase the challenges faced by those you serve and how your organization is

making a difference. Use vivid descriptions, personal anecdotes, and testimonials to create an emotional connection. When donors feel emotionally connected to your cause, they are more likely to engage and support your efforts.

Here are some examples of how you can effectively use storytelling in your donor communications:

- **Personal Testimonials:** Share personal stories of individuals or communities who have directly benefited from your organization's programs. Let the beneficiaries themselves share their experiences and how their lives have been transformed, adding a human touch to your appeals.

- **Donor Impact Stories:** Showcase the impact of donors' contributions through storytelling. Highlight specific projects or initiatives that were made possible by their support and how those projects have made a meaningful difference.

- **Founder's Story:** If your organization has an inspiring founder's story, share it with donors. Explain the motivation behind starting the organization, the challenges faced, and the ultimate vision that drives the work.

- **Visual Storytelling:** Use compelling visuals, such as photographs and videos, to tell stories that evoke emotions. A picture or video can often convey the impact of your work more effectively than words alone.

- **Narrative Case Studies:** Create in-depth case studies that walk donors through the journey of an individual or a family that your organization has helped. Highlight the challenges they faced, the support they received, and their transformation as a result.

- **Impact Reports:** Use data and storytelling together to demonstrate the scale of your organization's impact. Convert statistics and metrics into relatable stories that show how the collective effort of donors has brought about significant change.

- **Storytelling Events:** Organize storytelling events where beneficiaries, volunteers, or staff members can share their experiences firsthand with donors. These events can be powerful in forging personal connections.

- **Social Media Stories:** Utilize platforms like Instagram Stories or Facebook Live to share real-time updates and stories from the field. This offers donors an intimate glimpse into your organization's day-to-day efforts.

- **Seasonal Campaigns:** Customize your storytelling to align with seasonal campaigns or events. For example, during holidays, share stories of hope and gratitude to resonate with the spirit of giving.

- **Donor Journeys:** Share stories that take donors on a journey, starting from their initial involvement with your organization to the impact they've made over time. Show donors the value of their long-term commitment.

- **Interactive Storytelling:** Engage donors through interactive storytelling, where they can actively participate in decision-making or virtual experiences that simulate the beneficiaries' challenges.

Remember the key to having impact is stories need to be authentic, transparent, and ethical. Focus on the emotional resonance and authenticity of the stories, and avoid using overly sensational or manipulative tactics. When donors connect emotionally with your organization's work through storytelling, they are more likely to become advocates for your cause and provide ongoing support.

Element 5. Highlight Individual Stories:
While it's important to showcase the collective impact of your organization, don't underestimate the power of individual stories. Highlighting personal stories of those affected by your work creates a sense of empathy and relatability. Share stories of individuals whose lives have been transformed by your programs or services. Highlight their journey, struggles, and ultimate success. By humanizing your impact, donors can better connect with the cause and understand the difference they can make.

Personal Timeout (PT) - In reference to the two previous important elements, at a specific point in my capital campaign consulting process I used to share a true story (Lance's Story) with potential donors in my capital campaigns. The story involved a donor that had lost a son and realized too late that while all of the added medical expenses he had encountered were challenging, they were proof of life. His point was anything that is alive will require investment of finances, times and talent. While this story was an emotional 'punch to the gut' of listeners, just getting donors to shed some tears was not the point of using it. It was used to challenge any notions of, 'Why should I sacrifice for this particular vision or cause?' The story ended with the line,

'That's why I will always belong to a church that needs money. A living, growing, thriving church will always require the continual, consistent, and conscientious financial support of its members...' (The text of this story is in Appendix A.)

Long story, short - It's great to share true stories and touching anecdotes with donors but it's even better if you share a story that serves a fundraising genuine purpose.

Element 6. Communicate the Need:
In addition to sharing success stories, it's important to communicate the ongoing need for support. Donors want to know that their contributions are making a tangible difference and addressing real challenges. Clearly articulate the specific needs and challenges your organization faces and explain how donor support can help overcome them. By communicating the need effectively, you inspire donors to take action and become part of the solution.

Element 7. Be Transparent and Authentic:
Donors value transparency and authenticity. Be honest about your organization's goals, challenges, and how you utilize donor contributions. Avoid exaggerated claims or misleading information. Provide accurate data and facts to support your messaging. Authenticity builds trust and fosters a long-

term relationship with your donors. Share the progress, setbacks, and lessons learned along the way. Donors appreciate transparency and feel more connected when they understand the realities of your work.

Element 8. Tailor Messages to Different Donor Segments:
Recognize that not all donors are the same. Tailor your messaging to different donor segments based on their interests, giving history, and engagement level. Consider creating different versions of your messages to resonate with specific groups.

Let's look at some specific groups and see how we might employ this strategy -

New Donors:
- Welcome Message: Send a personalized welcome message expressing gratitude for their first-time donation and highlight the impact their support will make.
- Introduction to the Cause: Provide a brief overview of the organization's mission, key projects, and success stories to help new donors understand the organization's work better.

Major Donors:
- Personalized Communication: Reach out individually to major donors with handwritten notes or personalized emails,

acknowledging their significant contributions and the difference they are making.

- Exclusive Updates: Offer exclusive updates on high-impact projects and invite major donors to special events to deepen their engagement.

Monthly Donors:
- Thank-You and Progress Reports: Regularly thank monthly donors for their ongoing support and provide them with monthly progress reports on how their recurring contributions are making a difference.

Young Donors:
- Engage on Social Media: Connect with young donors through social media platforms, sharing engaging content and stories that align with their interests.
- Cause-Related Challenges: Organize cause-related challenges or campaigns that encourage young donors to take an active role in fundraising.

Legacy Donors (Planned Giving):
- Legacy Circle Updates: Create a dedicated newsletter or communication stream for legacy donors, updating them on the organization's long-term impact and how their planned gifts are making a lasting difference.

Geographic Segments:
- Local Impact Stories: For donors from specific regions, share success stories and initiatives that directly benefit their local communities.
- Tailored Events: Organize region-specific events to engage donors personally and connect them with beneficiaries in their area.

These are just a few of the groups that might exist within your donor base. A short brainstorming session might easily identify this many more!

***

Creating a donor communication plan that encompasses various channels and touchpoints

It is important to map out a communications strategy or plan for your donors. When will you connect with them? How often will you connect with them? What will be your message when you do connect with them? These communication elements should not be left to chance. Below is a sample donor communications plan. You will notice it utilizes various communication channels and specifies when a connection should be generated. This is not to say your organization needs each and every element shown here. But, hopefully you can see that using differing channels can reach different donors and donor segments. Feel free to use it as a model to develop a plan for your organization.

Donor Communication Plan: *Building Lasting Connections*

Goal: To engage donors effectively and cultivate long-term relationships by providing meaningful touchpoints across various communication channels.

Target Audience: Donors of all levels, including new donors, one-time donors, monthly donors, and major donors.

1. **Welcome and Thank-You Message** (Email):
   - Within 24 hours of a donation, send a personalized thank-you email to express immediate gratitude for their support. Provide a brief overview of the impact of their contribution and how it aligns with the organization's mission.

2. **Impactful Follow-Up** (Direct Mail):
   - Within one week of the initial thank-you email, send a handwritten note or a personalized direct mail piece, reiterating

the donor's importance and the specific outcomes their support has achieved.

3. **Monthly Newsletter** (Email):
  · Send a monthly newsletter featuring engaging content, including beneficiary stories, program updates, and upcoming events. Highlight different donor impact stories in each edition to demonstrate the collective power of giving.

4. **Personalized Progress Reports** (Direct Mail):
  · On a quarterly basis, send donors personalized impact reports detailing the results of their contributions. Include charts, infographics, and compelling visuals to show the tangible difference they have made.

5. **Exclusive Donor Events** (Virtual or In-Person):
  · Host quarterly exclusive events for major donors and monthly donors to connect with organizational leaders, program beneficiaries, and like-minded supporters. Offer a unique opportunity to witness the impact of their generosity firsthand.

6. **Social Media Engagement** (Facebook, Twitter, Instagram):
  · Maintain an active presence on social media platforms, sharing impactful

stories, behind-the-scenes content, and live updates from events. Regularly acknowledge and celebrate donors' contributions publicly.

7. **Personalized Phone Calls** (Phone):
   - Initiate personalized phone calls from board members or senior staff members to thank major donors or those who have been with the organization for a significant period. Show appreciation for their continued support and dedication.

8. **Text Message Updates** (SMS):
   - Send occasional text message updates to donors about time-sensitive campaigns, emergency response efforts, or exciting news related to their areas of interest.

9. **Annual Impact Report** (Printed and Digital):
   - At the end of the year, create a comprehensive annual impact report, showcasing the organization's achievements, testimonials from beneficiaries, and a tribute to donors' contributions. Send a printed version to major donors and a digital version to all donors.

10. **Giving Anniversary Acknowledgements** (Email/Direct Mail):

- Acknowledge donors' giving anniversaries with a special note of appreciation, recognizing their loyalty and commitment to the cause.

11. **Online Fundraising Campaigns** (Website and Email):
- Launch targeted online fundraising campaigns with specific goals and deadlines, leveraging the website and email communication to drive donor engagement.

12. **Survey and Feedback** (Email or Online Form):
- Regularly seek donors' feedback through surveys or online forms to understand their preferences, interests, and satisfaction with their donor experience. Use the insights to improve and refine the communication strategy.

By implementing this comprehensive donor communication plan, the organization can ensure donors feel valued, engaged, and inspired throughout their journey with the organization. The various touchpoints and channels provide ample opportunities to demonstrate the impact of donors' contributions and create a sense of community around the shared mission.

***

Designing effective fundraising appeals and campaigns

Designing effective fundraising appeals and campaigns is crucial for nonprofit organizations seeking to engage donors and generate support for their cause. A well-crafted appeal can inspire donors to take action, contribute to the organization, and drive fundraising success. In this section, we will explore the key components of designing effective fundraising appeals and campaigns that resonate with donors and motivate them to make a difference.

Component 1. Clearly Define Your Goal:
Before launching a fundraising appeal or campaign, it is essential to clearly define your goal. What specific outcome are you seeking to achieve? Are you raising funds for a specific program, project, or initiative? Defining a clear and compelling goal helps donors understand the purpose and impact of their contributions, motivating them to take action.

Component 2. Identify Your Target Audience:
To design effective fundraising appeals, it is crucial to identify your target audience. Who are the donors you are trying to reach?

Segment your donor base based on their interests, giving history, and engagement level. Tailor your messaging, tone, and communication channels to resonate with each specific group. By understanding your target audience, you can create appeals that speak directly to their motivations and aspirations.

Component 3. Craft a Compelling Story:

A powerful storytelling element is the cornerstone of an effective fundraising appeal. Craft a compelling narrative that showcases the impact of your organization's work. Share real-life stories of individuals or communities that have been positively affected by your programs or services. Use emotional language, vivid descriptions, and personal anecdotes to create an emotional connection with donors. A well-told story helps donors understand the importance of their support and inspires them to make a difference.

Component 4. Communicate Urgency and Need:

In fundraising appeals, it is crucial to communicate a sense of urgency and need. Clearly articulate why donor support is needed now and the specific challenges or opportunities your organization is facing. Use compelling statistics, data, and evidence to demonstrate the urgency of the situation. Donors are more likely to respond when they understand the pressing need and the impact their contributions can make.

Component 5. Utilize Emotional Appeals:
Emotions play a significant role in donor decision-making. Tap into the emotions of your donors by highlighting the positive impact they can make through their support. Appeal to their sense of empathy, compassion, and desire to create change. Use words and imagery that evoke feelings of hope, joy, or a desire to alleviate suffering. Emotional appeals help donors connect with your cause on a deeper level and inspire them to take action.

Component 6. Showcase Measurable Results:
Donors want to see tangible results and outcomes from their contributions. Clearly communicate the impact and results achieved through previous donations. Highlight specific achievements, milestones, or success stories to demonstrate the effectiveness of your organization's work. Sharing measurable results builds trust and confidence in your organization and encourages donors to continue supporting your cause.

Component 7. Create a Compelling Call-to-Action:
A compelling call-to-action is crucial to driving donor engagement and response. Clearly state what action you want donors to take, whether

it's making a donation, volunteering, or spreading the word. Use persuasive language and a sense of urgency to motivate donors to act immediately. Provide simple and convenient ways for donors to take action, such as online donation forms or pre-filled response cards.

Component 8. Utilize Multiple Communication Channels:

To reach a wider audience and maximize the impact of your fundraising appeals, utilize multiple communication channels. Consider using email, direct mail, social media, website, and personal outreach to engage donors. Each channel has its strengths and preferences, so diversifying your communication approach allows you to reach donors through their preferred channels. Ensure consistent messaging and branding across all channels for a cohesive donor experience.

Component 9. Incorporate Visuals and Design:

Visual elements can significantly enhance the effectiveness of your fundraising appeals. Utilize compelling visuals to communicate ideas, positive feelings, people involvement, etc. Use the broadest looking audience you can in your visual materials. Incorporate various genders, nationalities, races, etc., if your appeal warrants it. It's a fact that the more inclusive and representative your visuals are, the more a broad spectrum of people will buy into and support your mission and vision.

***

Leveraging digital platforms for donor engagement and communication

In today's digital age, nonprofit organizations have a wide range of digital platforms at their disposal to engage donors and communicate their mission effectively. Leveraging these platforms can significantly enhance donor engagement, expand reach, and drive fundraising success. In this section, we will explore the key strategies and best practices for leveraging digital platforms for donor engagement and communication.

Strategy 1. Build a Strong Online Presence:

To effectively leverage digital platforms, it is crucial to build a strong online presence. Start by creating a user-friendly and visually appealing website that showcases your organization's mission, impact, and ways to get involved. Ensure that your website is mobile-responsive to cater to donors who access it from various devices. Optimize your website for search engines to increase its visibility and reach.

Strategy 2. Engage on Social Media:
Social media platforms offer a powerful way to connect with donors and amplify your organization's message. Identify the social media platforms where your target audience is most active and create engaging profiles. Regularly share updates, success stories, photos, videos, and relevant news to keep donors informed and inspired. Encourage donors to share your content, follow your social media accounts, and actively participate in discussions.

Strategy 3. Use Email Marketing:
Email marketing remains one of the most effective digital communication channels for donor engagement. Build an email list of donors, volunteers, and supporters who have expressed interest in your organization. Segment your email list based on donor preferences, giving history, and engagement level to send targeted and personalized messages. Use compelling subject lines, concise and impactful content, and clear calls-to-action to drive donor response.

Strategy 4. Implement Peer-to-Peer Fundraising:
Peer-to-peer fundraising empowers donors to become advocates and fundraisers on behalf of your organization. Provide your supporters with the tools and resources they need to create their own fundraising campaigns on

digital platforms. Encourage them to share their campaign pages with their networks, leveraging the power of social connections to expand your reach and acquire new donors.

Strategy 5. Live Streaming and Virtual Events:

Digital platforms allow for engaging live streaming and virtual events, which can be powerful tools for donor engagement. Host webinars, panel discussions, Q&A sessions, or virtual galas to connect with donors in real-time. Incorporate interactive elements, such as live polls or Q&A sessions, to foster donor participation. Encourage virtual attendees to donate, share the event with their networks, and actively engage through comments and chat features.

Strategy 6. Online Giving Platforms:

Online giving platforms provide a convenient and secure way for donors to contribute to your organization. Partner with reputable online giving platforms that offer user-friendly interfaces, flexible donation options, and robust security measures. Ensure that your online giving platform is integrated with your website, making it easy for donors to find and donate to your cause. Provide clear instructions and options for recurring donations to encourage sustained support.

Strategy 7. Personalize Communication:

Digital platforms provide opportunities for personalized communication with donors. Utilize data and analytics to understand donor preferences, giving history, and interests. Send personalized messages and recommendations based on their past interactions and behaviors. Use donor names in email communications and tailor content to their specific areas of interest. Personalization shows donors that you value their individual support and helps foster stronger connections.

Strategy 8. Utilize Video Content:

Video content has become increasingly popular and engaging in the digital space. Create impactful videos that highlight your organization's mission, success stories, and impact. Share videos on your website, social media channels, and email campaigns to effectively convey your message and evoke emotion. Consider creating short testimonial videos from beneficiaries or heartfelt messages from your team to foster a deeper connection with donors.

Strategy 9. Encourage User-Generated Content:

User-generated content can be a powerful tool for donor engagement and communication. Encourage donors to share their experiences, their pictures, their stories on your digital channels.

In summary, crafting compelling donor communications is a critical skill for nonprofit organizations seeking to engage donors effectively and drive fundraising success. Knowing and understanding the strategies, techniques, and best practices necessary to create messages that resonate with donors, inspire action, and build lasting relationships will serve us and our organizations well.

Chapter 4 - Cultivating Donor-Centric Relationships

- **Building strong connections through personalized interactions**
- **Developing effective donor cultivation plans and strategies**
- **Implementing donor recognition and stewardship initiatives**

Welcome to chapter 4: Cultivating Donor-centric Relationships. In this chapter, we will explore the essential strategies and best practices for building and nurturing strong relationships with your donors. Cultivating donor-centric relationships is crucial for the long-term sustainability and success of nonprofit organizations. By developing meaningful connections with donors, you can foster loyalty, increase donor retention, and inspire continued support for your cause.

In this chapter, we will delve into various aspects of cultivating donor relationships, including effective stewardship, donor recognition, donor communication, and donor engagement. We will provide practical guidance and actionable steps to help you build genuine and lasting relationships with YOUR donors. Let's get started -

Building strong connections through personalized interactions

Building strong relationships with donors is work. It takes a personal investment of time and effort. And, some times in spite of our best efforts, the ROI doesn't seem to be compensatory to the energy expenditure. This can be frustrating but what's the alternative? Donor-centric relationships are the life-blood of any non-profit. Without donors we don't exist, at least not for long.

Here are six important principles to remember when it comes to building strong donor relationships. Use one or all of these to justify your investment of time and expenses with your Board or client when you're working on your next fundraising campaign :) -

Principle 1. The Importance of Donor Relationships:

Building strong relationships with donors goes beyond one-time transactions or donations. Cultivating donor relationships is about creating a sense of partnership, trust, and shared purpose. Donors who feel valued, appreciated, and connected to your organization are more likely to become long-term supporters and advocates for your cause. By investing time and effort in building donor relationships, you can create a community of passionate supporters who are committed to making a difference.

Principle 2. Effective Stewardship:

Stewardship is the process of managing and nurturing relationships with donors to ensure their continued engagement and support. In this section, we will explore strategies for effective stewardship, including timely and personalized thank-you messages, donor recognition programs, and ongoing communication. By practicing effective stewardship, you can demonstrate your organization's gratitude, keep donors informed about the impact of their contributions, and strengthen their commitment to your cause.

Principle 3. Donor Recognition:

Recognizing and appreciating donors is a crucial element of cultivating strong relationships. In this module, we will discuss different ways to recognize and acknowledge donors for their support. From personalized thank-you notes to donor appreciation events, we will explore creative and meaningful ways to express gratitude. By recognizing donors publicly and privately, you can make them feel valued, appreciated, and motivated to continue supporting your organization.

Principle 4. Donor Communication:

Effective communication is key to cultivating donor relationships. In this module, we will delve into the best practices for donor communication, including creating donor-centered messaging, storytelling, and utilizing various communication channels. We will discuss the importance of regular and consistent communication, tailored to donor preferences and interests. By establishing open and transparent lines of communication, you can foster a sense of trust and engagement with your donors.

Principle 5. Donor Engagement:

Donor engagement goes beyond financial contributions. It involves creating meaningful opportunities for donors to connect with your organization, its mission, and the communities you serve. In this module, we will explore strategies for donor engagement, including volunteer programs, events, and advocacy opportunities. We will discuss the benefits of involving donors in your organization's activities and providing them with a sense of purpose and impact.

Principle 6. Building Trust and Transparency:

Trust and transparency are fundamental in cultivating strong donor relationships. In this module, we will explore how to build trust by being transparent about your organization's goals, financials, and impact. We will discuss the importance of sharing progress, challenges, and successes with your donors. By fostering an environment of trust and transparency, you can strengthen donor relationships and inspire confidence in your organization's work.

***

Developing Effective Donor Cultivation Plans and Strategies

Donor cultivation is the process of building and strengthening relationships with donors to inspire ongoing engagement and support. Cultivating donors is a critical aspect of fundraising for nonprofit organizations, as it increases donor loyalty, encourages continued giving, and fosters a sense of partnership and shared purpose. To maximize the effectiveness of donor cultivation efforts, it is essential to develop well-defined plans and strategies. In this section, we will explore the key steps involved in developing effective donor cultivation plans and strategies.

Step 1. Set Clear Goals and Objectives:

Before embarking on donor cultivation, it is crucial to establish clear goals and objectives. These goals should align with your organization's overall fundraising objectives and mission. Identify what you want to achieve through donor cultivation, whether it's increasing donor retention, securing larger donations, or expanding your donor base. By setting specific and measurable goals, you can track progress and evaluate the success of your cultivation efforts.

Step 2. Segment Your Donor Base:

Not all donors are the same, and tailoring your cultivation efforts to different segments of your donor base can significantly enhance their effectiveness. Segment donors based on factors such as giving history, interests, motivations, and engagement level. This segmentation allows you to create more targeted and personalized cultivation strategies for each group. By understanding the unique needs and preferences of each donor segment, you can deliver more relevant and impactful cultivation experiences.

Step 3. Research and Data Analysis:
Conduct comprehensive research and data analysis to gain insights into your donors. This includes analyzing giving patterns, demographics, past interactions, and areas of interest. Utilize donor management software or customer relationship management (CRM) systems to track and manage donor data effectively. The research and data analysis process helps you understand donor behavior, identify trends, and make informed decisions when developing cultivation strategies. It enables you to tailor your approaches based on data-driven insights.

Step 4. Develop a Donor Cultivation Plan:
A well-structured cultivation plan provides a roadmap for effectively engaging and nurturing relationships with donors. Outline the specific strategies, activities, and touch-points that will be implemented to cultivate donors. Consider incorporating a mix of personal interactions, targeted communications, events, and stewardship activities. Include a timeline for each cultivation activity to ensure consistent engagement throughout the year. Your cultivation plan should be flexible enough to accommodate different donor segments and allow for adjustments based on donor feedback and preferences.

Step 5. Personalized Stewardship and Communication:

Stewardship plays a vital role in donor cultivation. Develop personalized stewardship strategies that recognize and appreciate donors for their contributions. This includes timely and meaningful thank-you messages, personalized acknowledgments, and recognition activities tailored to each donor segment. Additionally, implement personalized communication strategies that address donor interests, motivations, and preferred communication channels. Use personalized content to keep donors informed about the impact of their contributions and the organization's progress.

Step 6. Engage in Face-to-Face Interactions:

Face-to-face interactions are powerful tools for cultivating strong donor relationships. Develop strategies for engaging donors in personal meetings, whether it's one-on-one meetings, small group gatherings, or cultivation events. These interactions provide opportunities to deepen connections, understand donor interests and motivations, and showcase the impact of their support. Face-to-face interactions allow for active listening, relationship-building, and the identification of new opportunities for engagement and support.

Step 7. Provide Meaningful Engagement Opportunities:

Create meaningful opportunities for donors to engage with your organization beyond financial contributions. Offer volunteering opportunities, participation in program activities, or involvement in advisory committees or boards. By involving donors in your organization's mission and programs, you give them a sense of ownership and deeper connection. Meaningful engagement opportunities reinforce their commitment to your cause and create ambassadors who can advocate for your organization.

Step 8. Measure and Evaluate:

Regularly measure and evaluate the effectiveness of your donor cultivation strategies. The old saying is, What gets measured gets done. And there is a lot of truth in it. How do you know if you're improving unless you measure and evaluate from time to time?

Unfortunately donors, like money, don't grow on trees. But, like trees, to be productive and fruitful, they have to be cultivated. Once you find a donor, take the time and effort necessary to cultivate them. Get to know them. Understand their reasons for wanting to be a part of your organization's mission and vision. With just occasional tending and watering, you'll discover a good donor can be fruitful to your non-profit for years to come.

***

Implementing Donor Recognition and Stewardship Initiatives

Donor recognition and stewardship initiatives are critical components of building and maintaining strong relationships with donors. Recognizing and appreciating donors for their contributions and demonstrating effective stewardship can inspire continued support, enhance donor satisfaction, and foster long-term engagement. In this section, we will explore the importance of donor recognition and stewardship and provide strategies for implementing effective initiatives.

The Importance of Donor Recognition

Donor recognition is about acknowledging and expressing gratitude to donors for their generosity and support. It is an essential aspect of donor-centric fundraising, as it shows donors that their contributions are valued and appreciated. Recognition not only strengthens the bond between donors and your organization but also motivates donors to continue their support. When donors feel recognized, they are more likely to become repeat donors, increase their giving, and even become advocates for your cause.

Tailoring Recognition to Donor Preferences

Effective donor recognition begins with understanding and respecting donor preferences. Some donors may prefer public recognition, while others may value more private gestures of appreciation. Take the time to learn about each donor's preferences through surveys, conversations, or data analysis. Tailor your recognition efforts accordingly, ensuring that they align with the comfort level and preferences of individual donors. This personalized approach demonstrates that you value and respect each donor as an individual.

Timely and Meaningful Thank-You Messages

One of the simplest yet most powerful forms of recognition is a sincere thank-you message. Ensure that your organization has a system in place to send timely and personalized thank-you messages to donors. These messages should go beyond a generic template and reflect the impact of the donor's contribution. Consider including specific details about how their support has made a difference and expressing gratitude for their ongoing commitment. Timely and meaningful thank-you messages demonstrate appreciation and reinforce the value of donors' contributions.

Donor Recognition Levels
Implementing a donor recognition level system can be an effective way to acknowledge donors at different giving levels. Establish recognition levels that reflect the impact of donors' contributions and create corresponding benefits or privileges. This could include listing donors' names in annual reports, on your website, or in promotional materials. Higher-level donors could receive additional recognition, such as exclusive events or personalized experiences. Donor recognition levels provide a structured approach to acknowledge and appreciate donors based on their giving capacity.

Personal Timeout (PT) - Donor recognition can be tricky at times. Some donors do not want public recognition or *any* recognition for that matter. Others, desire public recognition but don't want to *appear* to desire recognition... Go figure. Sometimes the organization struggles to find an acceptable way to give the appropriate recognition. I worked with a church that wanted to build a new Family Life Center. This is typically a multi-purpose building that allows a church to conduct events, dinners, youth gatherings, etc. During the capital campaign, a potential significant donor had approached the church's pastor about making a sizable gift. It would have paid well over half of the new building's costs. The only caveat - the donor wanted the building named after his mother; Something like the 'Lois Jones Family Life Center.' The pastor pondered this prospect but eventually decided he could not accept the gift under those conditions. He feared it would upset other members of his congregation who might not want anybody's name attached to the building. Decide ahead of time what types of recognition are acceptable and what kinds of recognition aren't going to work for you.

Donor Recognition Events

Organizing donor recognition events can create a special and memorable experience for your supporters. These events can range from small gatherings to larger galas, depending on your organization's capacity and donor base. Recognize donors publicly during these events, highlighting their contributions and sharing success stories that demonstrate the impact of their support. Donor recognition events offer opportunities for donors to connect with each other, organizational leaders, and program beneficiaries, fostering a sense of community and shared purpose.

Recognition events allow nonprofits to express gratitude in a more individual and tangible manner, creating a sense of pride and fulfillment for donors who can see the impact of their contributions firsthand. This acknowledgment goes beyond a simple "thank you" and helps foster a deeper connection between the organization and its supporters. Donor recognition events help bridge the gap between the donor and the organization, creating a sense of belonging and involvement that goes beyond the act of giving.

Donor recognition events can serve as educational platforms, allowing organizations to share updates, progress reports, and future plans with their donors. These events provide an opportunity to communicate the organization's achievements, highlight ongoing projects, and outline future goals.

Lastly, donor recognition events can serve as a means to build and strengthen relationships with donors. These events provide a platform for nonprofits to engage with donors on a more personal level, enabling face-to-face interactions and networking opportunities. By bringing donors together, organizations can create a community of like-minded individuals who share a passion for a common cause. Building these relationships fosters loyalty and trust, encouraging donors to continue their support and potentially increase their contributions over time.

Personalized Donor Impact Reports

Donor impact reports are powerful tools for recognizing donors and showing the tangible outcomes of their contributions. Develop personalized reports that detail the specific projects, programs, or initiatives that donors have supported. Include stories, photos, and testimonials that illustrate the impact of their donations. By showcasing the results of their generosity, you reinforce the value and importance of their contributions. Personalized donor impact reports demonstrate transparency and accountability while deepening donors' understanding of your organization's work.

Donors want to know how their contributions are being utilized and the real-world difference they are making. A personalized report enables organizations to demonstrate exactly how the donor's funds have been allocated and the specific outcomes achieved as a result. This level of openness builds trust and confidence, as donors can see firsthand the impact of their giving.

Furthermore, personalized donor impact reports offer a unique opportunity to create a personal connection between the donor and the beneficiaries of their support. By sharing individual stories, testimonials, or case studies, these reports humanize the impact of the donor's contributions. Donors can see how their generosity has directly improved the lives of individuals or communities, creating a sense of fulfillment and purpose. This personal connection deepens the emotional bond between the donor and the cause, encouraging ongoing support and potentially inspiring additional giving.

Finally, personalized donor impact reports provide an opportunity for organizations to express their gratitude and appreciation for the donor's support. By acknowledging the donor's specific contributions, the report shows that their commitment has not gone unnoticed. This recognition goes beyond a generic "thank you" and demonstrates a deeper understanding of the donor's individual impact. Donors who feel genuinely appreciated are more likely to continue their support and potentially increase their level of giving in the future.

Ongoing Communication and Updates

Effective stewardship involves maintaining consistent and meaningful communication with donors. Regularly update donors on your organization's activities, accomplishments, and challenges. Share stories of individuals or communities impacted by their support. Utilize various communication channels such as email, newsletters, social media, and annual reports to keep donors informed. Ongoing communication demonstrates transparency, builds trust, and reinforces the connection between donors and your organization.

Chapter 5 - Maximizing Fundraising Results

- **Leveraging donor feedback to enhance fundraising strategies**
- **Employing effective donor acquisition and retention techniques**
- **Evaluating and optimizing fundraising efforts for long-term success**

Welcome to Chapter 5 of our study of donor-focused fundraising. In this section, we will explore strategies and techniques to maximize your fundraising results. Fundraising is a critical aspect of nonprofit organizations, and the ability to generate significant financial support is vital for achieving your mission and creating a lasting impact. This module will provide you with insights, tools, and best practices to optimize your fundraising efforts and achieve outstanding results.

Before diving into specific strategies, it's essential to understand what makes fundraising efforts effective. Fundraising effectiveness goes beyond simply raising money. It involves engaging and inspiring donors, building long-term relationships, and achieving sustainable financial support. In this section, we will explore key indicators of fundraising effectiveness, such as donor retention rates, donor acquisition costs, average gift size, and overall return on investment. By understanding these metrics, you will be better equipped to assess and enhance the performance of your fundraising efforts.

To maximize fundraising results, it is crucial to develop a comprehensive fundraising plan. This plan should align with your organization's goals and mission while considering the specific needs and interests of your donor base. In this module, we will guide you through the process of creating a well-defined fundraising plan that includes specific strategies, target audiences, timelines, and resource allocation. A comprehensive plan provides clarity and direction, ensuring that your fundraising efforts are focused and aligned with your organization's objectives.

Segmenting your donor base is a fundamental practice for maximizing fundraising results. Not all donors are the same, and tailoring your strategies to different segments can significantly enhance your outcomes. In this module, we will explore various donor segmentation approaches, such as giving history, donor interests, and engagement level. By understanding the unique characteristics and preferences of each segment, you can customize your messaging, appeals, and stewardship efforts to resonate with donors on a more personal level.

In today's digital age, fundraising efforts should extend beyond traditional methods. Implementing multi-channel fundraising strategies allows you to reach donors through various platforms and channels, including online fundraising campaigns, social media, direct mail, events, and peer-to-peer fundraising. In this module, we will discuss the benefits and best practices of each channel and explore how to integrate them effectively to maximize fundraising results. By diversifying your fundraising approaches, you can engage donors through their preferred communication channels and maximize your reach.

Crafting compelling and effective fundraising appeals is crucial for driving donor action and generating financial support. In this section, we will delve into the art of creating impactful appeals that resonate with your donors' emotions and motivations. We will explore storytelling techniques, leveraging donor testimonials, and utilizing persuasive language to capture donors' attention and inspire them to take action. By understanding the elements of a successful appeal, you can create powerful messages that connect with your donors and drive them to support your cause.

Building and nurturing strong relationships with your donors is essential for maximizing fundraising results. In this module, we will explore effective donor relationship management strategies. This includes implementing donor stewardship initiatives, providing personalized communication and recognition, and engaging donors in ongoing dialogue. We will also discuss the importance of regular donor engagement activities, such as events, volunteer opportunities, and exclusive benefits. By focusing on donor relationship management, you can cultivate loyalty and foster long-term support from your donors.

To maximize fundraising results, it is crucial to continuously monitor and evaluate your efforts.

***

Leveraging donor feedback to enhance fundraising strategies

In the world of fundraising, donor feedback is a valuable asset that can provide valuable insights and shape the success of your fundraising strategies. Donors are essential stakeholders in your organization, and their perspectives, preferences, and experiences can offer a wealth of information to help you improve and optimize your fundraising efforts. In this chapter, we explore the importance of leveraging donor feedback and provide strategies for effectively collecting, analyzing, and implementing donor feedback to enhance your fundraising strategies.

- Recognizing the Value of Donor Feedback: Donor feedback is a valuable resource that can inform your fundraising strategies and decisions. By actively seeking and listening to donor feedback, you demonstrate your commitment to donor satisfaction and your willingness to improve their experience. Donors' feedback can provide insights into their motivations for giving, their preferred communication channels, and their perceptions of your organization's impact. This knowledge enables you to tailor your fundraising strategies to better meet donors' needs and expectations.

- Creating Feedback Channels: To effectively leverage donor feedback, it is important to establish clear and accessible channels for donors to provide their input. Create opportunities for donors to share their thoughts, ideas, and concerns. This can be done through surveys, feedback forms on your website, focus groups, or one-on-one conversations. Make it easy for donors to provide feedback by ensuring that the channels are user-friendly, convenient, and secure. By providing multiple feedback channels, you can accommodate different donor preferences and increase the likelihood of receiving valuable insights.

- Designing Effective Feedback Surveys:

Surveys are a common and effective method for collecting donor feedback. When designing surveys, keep them concise, clear, and focused on gathering actionable information. Ask specific questions related to donors' experiences, satisfaction levels, motivations, and suggestions for improvement. Utilize a mix of closed-ended and open-ended questions to gather both quantitative and qualitative feedback. Consider using rating scales or Likert scales to measure satisfaction levels or likelihood to recommend. By designing effective surveys, you can gather relevant and meaningful data to inform your fundraising strategies.

- Listening and Responding to Feedback:

Collecting donor feedback is only the first step. It is equally important to actively listen and respond to the feedback received. Acknowledge the time and effort donors put into providing their input and express gratitude for their feedback. Take the time to review and analyze the feedback, identifying common themes, trends, and areas for improvement. Once you have analyzed the feedback, develop a plan for addressing the concerns raised and implementing changes based on the suggestions provided. When donors see that their feedback is valued and acted upon, it fosters trust and strengthens the donor-organization relationship.

- Tailoring Fundraising Strategies: Donor feedback can provide valuable insights that can inform and shape your fundraising strategies. Analyze the feedback to identify patterns and trends that can guide your decision-making. For example, if donors express a preference for receiving updates through social media platforms, you can allocate more resources to social media fundraising campaigns. If donors mention a desire for more engagement opportunities, consider developing volunteer programs or exclusive events. By tailoring your fundraising strategies to align with donor preferences, you can increase donor engagement and enhance the effectiveness of your fundraising efforts.

- Enhancing Donor Communication:
Donor feedback can offer valuable insights into how to improve your communication strategies. Pay attention to donors' feedback on the clarity, frequency, and relevance of

your communications. Are there specific communication channels or formats that donors prefer? Do they find the content engaging and informative? Use this feedback to enhance your communication efforts, ensuring that your messages are compelling, personalized, and delivered through the channels preferred by your donors. Effective communication builds trust, fosters engagement, and increases the likelihood of donor support.

***

Employing effective donor acquisition and retention techniques

Donor acquisition and retention are two crucial components of successful fundraising for nonprofit organizations. While acquiring new donors is essential for expanding your donor base, retaining existing donors is equally important for sustained support and long-term impact. In this section, we will explore effective techniques for donor acquisition and retention that can help you build a strong and loyal donor community.

Donor acquisition refers to the process of attracting and converting new donors to support your organization's mission. To effectively acquire new donors, it is important to have a clear understanding of your target audience. Identify the individuals or groups who are most likely to resonate with your cause and align with your organization's values. Conduct market research, analyze demographics, and consider the interests and motivations of potential donors. By understanding your target audience, you can tailor your fundraising strategies to effectively reach and engage them.

To attract new donors, you need to articulate a compelling case for support. Clearly communicate your organization's mission, vision, and the impact of your work. Emphasize the unique value proposition of your organization and explain why donors' support is crucial. Tell compelling stories that illustrate the tangible outcomes of your programs and the difference donors can make by contributing to your cause. A well-crafted case for support resonates with potential donors and motivates them to take action.

Employing multi-channel fundraising techniques is crucial for effective donor acquisition. Utilize a variety of channels and platforms to reach potential donors. This includes online platforms, direct mail, events, social media, and peer-to-peer fundraising. Each channel offers unique opportunities to engage with different segments of your target audience. By diversifying your fundraising approaches, you can maximize your reach and connect with potential donors through their preferred communication channels.

Encourage your current donors to become ambassadors for your organization by setting up personal fundraising pages and reaching out to their friends, family, and colleagues. Provide them with the necessary tools, resources, and guidance to effectively advocate for your cause. Peer-to-peer fundraising is a powerful strategy for donor acquisition. It involves leveraging the networks and connections of your existing donors to attract new supporters. Peer-to-peer fundraising expands your reach and allows potential donors to connect with your organization through trusted relationships.

Acquiring new donors is just the first step; building relationships is crucial for long-term engagement and retention. As new donors come on board, make sure to prioritize relationship-building efforts. Thank them promptly and sincerely for their support, and provide personalized communication to make them feel valued. Develop stewardship strategies that demonstrate the impact of their contributions and keep them informed about your organization's progress. Building strong relationships from the start sets the foundation for ongoing engagement and future support.

Donor retention is closely tied to effective donor stewardship. Stewardship refers to the ongoing efforts to engage, recognize, and appreciate donors. Implement a comprehensive stewardship program that recognizes donors' contributions and demonstrates the impact of their support. This can include personalized thank-you messages, donor recognition events, exclusive benefits for donors, and regular updates on your organization's work. Effective stewardship shows donors that their support is valued and reinforces their connection to your cause, increasing the likelihood of continued engagement and support.

Personal Timeout (PT) - Donor retention is critical in terms of longterm organizational success. (*This is the single most frequent question I get from perspective clients - How can we find new donors?*) Yet, retention of *all* donors is unlikely and nearly impossible. In my work with over 5,000 churches a very real statistic is each church will lose approximately twenty percent of their donors each year. This creates a couple of issues - First, if you are not aware of this stat when you begin to measure it and discover this statistic, you may panic. 20%? Aaahhh! But, this is the norm for 99% of these organizations annually. Donors leave for a variety of reasons and they are not all negative. Some donors move away, others pass away. Not much you can do about either of these situations. Some donors get sideways with the mission/vision of the organization or the organization's leadership. Expect and accept that these things will happen. But that brings us to the second issue - once you become aware of this KPI you have to strategize on how you are going to replace these donors that leave each year. If there is no replacement, you are out of business within five years...

Boomerang suggests based on their studies that average donor retention for non-religious non-profits hovers between 40-45% annually. This means if 100 donors give your organization a gift this year, only 40-45 of them will give again next year. (https://bloomerang.co/blog/donor-retention/)

Donors have unique preferences when it comes to communication and engagement. Tailor your communication strategies to match the preferences of individual donors. Some may prefer email updates, while others may appreciate direct mail or phone calls. Utilize donor management systems to track communication preferences and interactions.

***

Evaluating and optimizing fundraising efforts for long-term success

In the dynamic landscape of fundraising, evaluation and optimization play a vital role in achieving long-term success. Regularly assessing the effectiveness of your fundraising efforts allows you to identify strengths, weaknesses, and areas for improvement. By optimizing your strategies based on data-driven insights, you can enhance your fundraising outcomes and maximize your organization's impact. In this section, we will explore the importance of evaluating fundraising efforts and provide strategies for optimizing your fundraising activities for long-term success.

1. Setting Clear and Measurable Goals:
To evaluate and optimize your fundraising efforts, it is essential to establish clear and measurable goals. Define specific objectives that align with your organization's mission and vision. These goals should be quantifiable and time-bound, allowing you to track progress and measure success. Examples of measurable goals include increasing the number of donors, improving donor retention rates, or raising a specific amount of funds. Clear goals provide a

benchmark for evaluation and guide the optimization process.

2. Tracking Key Performance Indicators:
Key Performance Indicators (KPIs) are measurable metrics that reflect the success of your fundraising efforts. Identify the relevant KPIs for your organization and track them regularly. Common KPIs include donor retention rate, donor acquisition cost, average gift size, fundraising ROI, and donor engagement levels. Tracking these indicators enables you to monitor the performance of your fundraising activities and identify trends or patterns that require attention. It also helps you make data-driven decisions when optimizing your strategies.

3. Analyzing Data and Feedback:
Data analysis is a critical component of evaluating fundraising efforts. Collect and analyze data from various sources, including donor databases, fundraising software, surveys, and feedback forms. Look for trends, patterns, and insights that can inform your decision-making. For example, analyze donor giving patterns to identify peak donation times or popular fundraising campaigns. Additionally, consider soliciting feedback from donors through surveys or focus groups to gain insights into their experiences and preferences. Analyzing data and feedback provides valuable information for optimizing your strategies.

4. Identifying Strengths and Weaknesses:
Evaluation allows you to identify the strengths and weaknesses of your fundraising efforts. Assess your organization's strengths, such as effective donor stewardship, compelling storytelling, or strong community partnerships. These strengths can serve as a foundation for optimizing your strategies. Simultaneously, identify areas that require improvement, such as low donor retention rates, limited donor engagement, or ineffective communication channels. Recognizing weaknesses helps you focus your optimization efforts on areas with the most significant potential for improvement.

5. Implementing A/B Testing:
A/B testing, also known as split testing, is a valuable technique for optimizing fundraising strategies. It involves comparing two versions of a fundraising campaign or appeal to determine which performs better. For example, you can test different variations of a fundraising email by changing the subject line, call-to-action, or storytelling approach. Split your donor database into two groups and send each version to separate segments. Analyze the response rates, donation amounts, and engagement levels to determine the more effective approach. A/B testing allows you to fine-tune your strategies based on real-time data and donor preferences.

6. Cultivating Donor Relationships:
Donor relationships are at the core of successful fundraising. Evaluation provides an opportunity to assess the strength of your donor relationships and identify areas for improvement. Regularly evaluate the effectiveness of your donor stewardship initiatives, such as thank-you messages, donor recognition events, and personalized communication. Seek feedback from donors on their satisfaction levels and their perceptions of your organization's engagement efforts. Use this information to enhance your relationship-building strategies and create meaningful connections with donors.

Fundraising is a dynamic field, and success requires adaptability and a willingness to learn from both successes and failures.

Chapter 6 - Ethical Considerations in Donor-Centric Fundraising

- **Exploring ethical guidelines and regulations in fundraising**
- **Ensuring transparency and accountability in donor relations**
- **Building trust and maintaining donor privacy and confidentiality**

Welcome to chapter 6 of our fundraising training program, where we will explore the crucial topic of ethical considerations in donor-focused fundraising. As fundraising professionals, we have a responsibility to uphold the highest ethical standards to ensure the trust, transparency, and long-term sustainability of our organizations. This module will delve into the ethical principles and practices that should guide our fundraising efforts, with a particular focus on prioritizing the well-being and interests of our donors.

Ethics in donor-focused fundraising go beyond legal compliance. While laws and regulations provide a framework for ethical behavior, they do not capture the full scope of what it means to act ethically in our interactions with donors. Ethical fundraising requires a deep understanding of the impact our actions have on donors, as well as a commitment to fairness, honesty, and respect.

Throughout this chapter, we will examine key ethical considerations in donor-focused fundraising and provide practical guidance for navigating complex situations. We will explore topics such as donor consent and privacy, transparency in fundraising practices, responsible donor acquisition, and the ethical use of donor data. By addressing these ethical considerations, we can foster strong, trust-based relationships with our donors and ensure the sustainability and reputation of our organizations.

Chapter 6 will also emphasize the importance of aligning our fundraising practices with the values and mission of our organizations. Ethical fundraising is not just a checklist of rules to follow but a commitment to values-driven decision-making. We will explore how to integrate ethical considerations into our fundraising strategies and ensure that our actions reflect the core values of our organizations.

In addition to ethical principles, we will examine the role of ethical leadership in fundraising. Ethical leaders set the tone for an organization's fundraising practices, championing ethical behavior, and creating a culture of transparency and accountability. We will discuss strategies for fostering ethical leadership within our organizations and promoting a strong ethical foundation in all aspects of our fundraising efforts.

Ultimately, this chapter aims to equip you with the knowledge and tools to navigate ethical challenges in donor-focused fundraising. By understanding and embracing ethical considerations, we can build stronger, more meaningful relationships with our donors and foster a culture of trust and integrity within our organizations.

We encourage you to engage actively with the content, reflect on your own fundraising practices, and consider how you can integrate ethical considerations into your daily work. By doing so, we can collectively elevate the standards of donor-focused fundraising and create a positive impact on the communities and causes we serve.

Get ready to dive into the ethical considerations that underpin donor-focused fundraising. Let's begin this chapter with a commitment to upholding the highest ethical standards and ensuring that our fundraising efforts prioritize the well-being and interests of our valued donors.

***

Exploring ethical guidelines and regulations in fundraising

Ethics and integrity are fundamental pillars of effective fundraising practices. As fundraising professionals, it is essential to navigate the complexities of ethical considerations and adhere to relevant guidelines and regulations. In this article, we will explore the importance of ethical guidelines and regulations in fundraising and discuss their implications for donor-focused efforts.

Ethical guidelines provide a framework for ethical decision-making, helping fundraising professionals maintain transparency, trust, and accountability in their interactions with donors. These guidelines are typically developed and promoted by professional associations, such as the Association of Fundraising Professionals (AFP) or the International Statement of Ethical

Principles in Fundraising. Let's delve into the key ethical guidelines commonly followed in fundraising:

1. Honesty and Transparency:

Honesty and transparency are foundational ethical principles in fundraising. Fundraisers must accurately represent their organizations and programs, ensuring that donors have a clear understanding of how their contributions will be used. Fundraisers should provide truthful information about the impact of donations and avoid misleading or deceptive practices. Transparency extends to financial reporting, ensuring that financial information is presented accurately and honestly.

2. Donor Privacy and Confidentiality:

Respecting donor privacy is critical in maintaining trust and fostering long-term relationships. Fundraisers must handle donor information confidentially and securely, adhering to relevant data protection laws and regulations. Donors should have control over the use of their personal information and be provided with options to opt out of communications or limit the sharing of their data. Transparency about data practices and adherence to privacy regulations are essential in building and maintaining trust with donors.

3. Informed Consent:

Informed consent is a crucial ethical consideration when soliciting donations. Donors should have a clear understanding of how their personal information will be used and shared. Fundraisers should obtain explicit consent from donors for specific communication channels, frequency, and purposes. Donors should also have the opportunity to opt out or unsubscribe from communications at any time. Informed consent empowers donors to make informed decisions about their engagement with the organization.

4. Responsible Donor Acquisition:

Ethical fundraising requires responsible donor acquisition practices. Fundraisers should engage in ethical prospect research and ensure that donor lists are obtained through legitimate means. Avoiding intrusive or misleading acquisition tactics is essential to maintain the integrity of the fundraising process. Organizations should prioritize engaging with individuals who have expressed interest in their cause or have a connection to their mission.

5. Avoiding Conflict of Interest:

Fundraisers should strive to avoid conflicts of interest that may compromise their impartiality or the best interests of the organization and its donors. Personal relationships or financial interests that could influence fundraising decisions should be disclosed and managed appropriately. Fundraisers should always prioritize the interests of the organization and act in a manner that preserves the trust and confidence of donors.

Personal Timeout (PT) - A question that frequently comes up when you as a fundraiser speak to major donors is, 'How are you being compensated?" What they are asking is, "If I give a larger gift does that mean you make more money fee-wise?" Some fundraisers and fundraising companies price their services based on the percentage of money raised. On the surface this seems reasonable. Why shouldn't I benefit more if I can raise more money for my non-profit client? But, I've always believed that if I charge a flat, set, pre-determined fee for my services - one which I can live with and feel good about - I can take this question off the table. Significant donors want their dollars to go towards the cause they are supporting not put them in your professional fundraising pocket. Using a set fee for my services allows me to respond, "I get a flat fee. If you give more, it doesn't mean I make more. It means more money goes to and toward the change you want to see happen."

I have heard tales of donors that waited to pledge significant gifts until after the commitment phase of a capital campaign just to avoid paying the consultant more money. I understand why they are doing it and don't really blame them. Make this a non-issue by charging a flat, predetermined fee for your services regardless of the amount raised. If you raise way more than expected, your client will feel they got a bargain by using you. And, if they feel that way, you'll likely be their first choice when it comes to hiring a fundraising professional in the future!

6. Professional Competence and Continuous Learning: Ethical fundraising requires ongoing professional development and the pursuit of knowledge. Fundraisers should strive to stay updated on best practices, legal requirements, and emerging ethical considerations in the field. Continuous learning enables fundraisers to adapt to changing landscapes and make informed decisions that prioritize the interests of donors and the organization.

While ethical guidelines provide general principles, it is equally important to understand and comply with the legal and regulatory frameworks governing fundraising activities. Compliance with applicable laws and regulations ensures ethical fundraising practices and protects the organization's reputation. Some common legal and regulatory areas to consider include:

1. Tax and Charitable Solicitation Laws: Fundraisers must comply with tax laws related to charitable contributions and solicitations. This may include registration and reporting requirements with tax authorities, disclosure obligations, and adherence to specific regulations governing fundraising activities.

2. Data Protection and Privacy Laws: Data protection and privacy regulations, such as the General Data Protection Regulation (GDPR) or the California Consumer Privacy Act (CCPA).

***

Ensuring Transparency and Accountability in Donor Relations

Transparency and accountability are essential pillars of effective donor relations. Donors place their trust and confidence in organizations when making contributions, and it is our responsibility as fundraisers to uphold their trust by demonstrating transparency and accountability in our interactions. In this section, we will explore the importance of transparency and accountability in donor relations and discuss strategies for fostering a culture of openness and trust.

1. Building Trust through Transparent Communication: Transparent communication is the foundation of strong donor relations.

Organizations should strive to be open and honest in their communication with donors. This involves providing clear and accurate information about the organization's mission, goals, programs, and financials. Donors should have access to information that allows them to make informed decisions about their contributions. Regular communication, such as impact reports or newsletters, helps keep donors informed about the organization's activities and the impact of their support.

2. Financial Transparency: Donors want assurance that their contributions are being used responsibly and effectively. Demonstrating financial transparency is crucial in building trust and accountability. Organizations should provide comprehensive financial reports, including audited financial statements, that clearly show how funds are allocated and spent. Financial transparency also includes disclosing administrative costs, fundraising expenses, and programmatic outcomes. Donors appreciate organizations that can demonstrate fiscal responsibility and show how their contributions make a difference.

3. Donor Stewardship and Reporting:
Stewardship is an ongoing process of nurturing relationships with donors and demonstrating the impact of their support. Organizations should implement robust donor stewardship

practices, including timely and personalized acknowledgments of donations, regular updates on programmatic activities, and reports on the outcomes achieved through donor contributions. By keeping donors informed and engaged, organizations can foster a sense of ownership and accountability among donors.

4. Donor Feedback and Engagement: Engaging donors in meaningful ways is key to building transparency and accountability. Organizations should actively seek donor feedback, opinions, and suggestions. This can be done through surveys, focus groups, or individual conversations. By listening to donor perspectives, organizations can understand donor expectations, concerns, and preferences. Actively involving donors in decision-making processes or inviting them to participate in events or volunteer activities creates a sense of ownership and collaboration.

5. Donor Privacy and Consent: Respecting donor privacy and obtaining consent for communication and data usage are crucial aspects of accountability. Organizations must have clear privacy policies that outline how donor information is collected, stored, and used. Donors should have control over their personal data and be given options to manage their communication preferences. Organizations should also ensure that donor

data is securely protected to maintain donor trust and comply with relevant data protection laws.

6. Feedback Mechanisms and Complaint Resolution: Establishing feedback mechanisms and complaint resolution processes demonstrates an organization's commitment to transparency and accountability. Donors should have a clear avenue to express concerns, provide feedback, or lodge complaints. Organizations should establish a designated point of contact and ensure that all complaints are addressed promptly, fairly, and confidentially. Handling feedback and complaints with professionalism and transparency helps build trust and shows donors that their voices are heard and valued.

7. Independent Oversight and Governance:
Strong governance structures and independent oversight play a crucial role in ensuring transparency and accountability. Organizations should establish effective governance mechanisms, such as boards of directors or advisory committees, that provide oversight and guidance. These governing bodies should include individuals with diverse expertise and backgrounds who can provide objective perspectives. Independent audits by external professionals also help validate financial transparency and reassure donors that the organization operates with integrity.

8. Continuous Improvement and Evaluation: Accountability requires a commitment to continuous improvement and evaluation. Organizations should regularly assess their performance, impact, and donor relations practices. This can be done through internal evaluations, external assessments, or surveys. By analyzing feedback and evaluating their effectiveness, organizations can identify areas for improvement and implement changes that enhance donor relationships.

***

Building trust and maintaining donor
privacy and confidentiality

Building trust and maintaining donor privacy and confidentiality are paramount in donor-focused fundraising. Donors entrust organizations with their personal information and financial contributions. It is our responsibility to protect that trust by safeguarding their privacy and maintaining the confidentiality of their data. In this section, we will explore some strategies for building trust and ensuring the privacy and confidentiality of donor information.

1. Clear Privacy Policies and Practices:

Transparency is key in building trust with donors. Organizations should develop and communicate clear privacy policies that outline how donor information is collected, used, stored, and protected. These policies should explain the purpose of data collection, the types of information collected, and the measures in place to ensure data security. Providing donors with a comprehensive understanding of how their personal information will be handled fosters trust and demonstrates a commitment to their privacy.

2. Secure Data Management:
Organizations must prioritize data security to protect donor privacy. Implementing robust data management practices, such as encryption, firewalls, and secure servers, helps safeguard donor information from unauthorized access or breaches. Regular software updates and security audits are essential to ensure that data protection measures are up to date and effective. By demonstrating a strong commitment to data security, organizations can instill confidence in donors that their information is handled with care.

3. Donor Consent and Communication Preferences:
Respecting donor consent is crucial in maintaining donor privacy. Organizations should obtain explicit consent from donors regarding the collection, use, and sharing of

their personal information. Donors should have control over their communication preferences, including the frequency and channels of communication. Providing easy opt-out options and honoring donor preferences demonstrates respect for their privacy choices and helps foster trust in the organization's practices.

4. Staff Training and Confidentiality Agreements:
Maintaining donor confidentiality requires a culture of privacy awareness within the organization. All staff members should receive training on the importance of donor privacy and confidentiality, as well as the organization's privacy policies and practices. Staff members should sign confidentiality agreements to reinforce their commitment to protecting donor information. Ongoing training and reminders can help ensure that all staff members understand and adhere to privacy protocols.

5. Limited Access and Data Sharing:
Organizations should implement access controls to limit internal access to donor information to only those who require it for their specific roles. This reduces the risk of unauthorized disclosure or misuse of donor data. Additionally, organizations should exercise caution when sharing donor information with external parties, such as vendors or partners. Data sharing agreements

should be in place to ensure that external parties adhere to the same privacy standards and safeguards.

6. Donor Anonymity and Non-Disclosure:
Respecting donor anonymity and non-disclosure requests is essential in maintaining donor privacy. Some donors may prefer to remain anonymous, and organizations should honor these preferences. Donors who choose to remain anonymous should not be publicly identified or acknowledged without their explicit consent. Respecting donor anonymity builds trust and reassures donors that their privacy is a top priority.

7. Regular Privacy Audits and Compliance:
Organizations should conduct regular privacy audits to assess compliance with relevant privacy regulations and evaluate the effectiveness of privacy practices. These audits can help identify areas for improvement and ensure ongoing compliance with data protection laws. Organizations should also stay abreast of changes in privacy regulations and adjust their practices accordingly to maintain compliance and safeguard donor privacy.

8. Incident Response and Notification:
In the event of a data breach or privacy incident, organizations should have a well-defined incident response plan in place. This includes a clear process for assessing and

containing the breach, notifying affected individuals and authorities as required by law, and providing support and resources to affected donors. Timely and transparent communication in such situations helps maintain trust with donors, even in challenging circumstances.

Maintaining open lines of regular communication with donors is vital.

Personal Timeout (PT) - Donor privacy issues are tricky sometimes. If the wrong people are in charge they can weaponize giving information. I worked with a client once that had appointed a specific person to spearhead the Follow-up efforts after a successful capital campaign. A regular part of my campaign follow-up involves periodic review of the giving progress of donors. Without this information, any action you take is just shooting into the wind. You don't know if it will help or hurt your efforts. Anyway, this particular person was VERY reluctant to permit me to review the giving records. I understand this hesitancy and applaud it on a basic level. They see themselves as protecting the confidentiality of their donors. Commendable. But, this person's hesitancy went over and beyond. I finally had to get the leader of the organization to personally instruct this staffer to turn over the financial information to me.

Once he did I immediately understood why the Follow-up leader had been so reluctant - he himself had not participated in the campaign. He talked a good game but had no skin in it. He did not want the organization's leader or other staffers to know of his non-involvement. So, he tried to keep others from reviewing the giving information for fear of exposure. I successfully lobbied the leader to replace him unless he made some sort of commitment. To have someone in charge of Follow-up who wasn't actually participating is hypocritical to say the least.

Chapter 7 - Case Studies and Practical Exercises

C hapter 7 of our donor-focused fundraising journey takes a hands-on approach to learning by diving into real-world case studies and engaging in practical exercises. This section offers a valuable opportunity for readers to apply the knowledge and skills they have acquired throughout the book in a practical setting.

Understanding the principles and best practices of donor-focused fundraising is essential, but it is equally important to see how these concepts are implemented in real-life scenarios. In this chapter, we will explore a variety of case studies that highlight successful donor-focused fundraising strategies, as well as challenges and lessons learned. These case studies will cover different sectors, organization sizes, and fundraising goals, allowing participants to gain insights from diverse perspectives.

The case studies will provide a comprehensive view of how organizations have effectively engaged with donors, developed personalized fundraising campaigns, cultivated long-term relationships, and achieved remarkable fundraising results. Participants will have the opportunity to analyze the strategies employed by these organizations, evaluate their impact, and identify key takeaways that can be applied to their own fundraising initiatives.

In addition to case studies, this chapter will include practical exercises that encourage participants to put their knowledge into action. These exercises will simulate real-world fundraising scenarios, allowing participants to practice key skills, such as crafting compelling donor communications, designing effective fundraising appeals, or developing donor cultivation plans. Through these exercises, participants will gain hands-on experience and refine their fundraising strategies and techniques.

The combination of case studies and practical exercises in this module aims to bridge the gap between theory and practice, ensuring that participants develop a deep understanding of donor-focused fundraising and its application in real-life situations. By examining successful examples, analyzing strategies, and actively engaging in exercises, participants will strengthen their skills, enhance their critical thinking abilities, and be better equipped to address the challenges and opportunities in their own fundraising efforts.

Throughout this module, participants will have the opportunity to collaborate with their peers, share insights, and learn from one another's experiences. Engaging in discussions and group activities will further enrich the learning experience and provide a platform for exchanging ideas and best practices.

By the end of chapter 7, readers will have a comprehensive understanding of how donor-focused fundraising principles are put into practice, the ability to critically evaluate fundraising strategies, and the confidence to apply their knowledge and skills to their own fundraising initiatives. This module will empower participants to adapt and innovate in their fundraising efforts, ensuring sustainable and impactful donor engagement.

We encourage participants to actively engage in the case studies and practical exercises, share their perspectives, and embrace the opportunity to learn from real-world examples. Let us embark on this exciting journey of applying donor-focused fundraising concepts to practical scenarios and further elevate our fundraising practices.

***

Analyzing Real-World Examples of Donor-Focused Fundraisers

Analyzing real-world examples of donor-focused fundraisers provides valuable insights into successful strategies and practices that organizations have employed to engage donors effectively and achieve their fundraising goals. By examining these examples, we can gain inspiration and learn from the experiences of others in the field. Let's explore several real-world examples of donor-focused fundraisers and analyze the key factors that contributed to their success.

Case Study # 1

Charity: Water - Engaging Donors through Transparency and Impact:

Charity: Water is a nonprofit organization that focuses on providing clean and safe drinking water to people in developing countries. One of their key strategies is transparency and impact reporting. They use storytelling and technology to showcase the direct impact of donations, sharing stories of individuals and communities benefiting from clean water projects. By providing real-time updates and GPS coordinates of completed projects, they create a sense of transparency and accountability that resonates with donors, inspiring them to contribute and stay engaged.

Key Takeaway: Transparency and impact reporting can build trust and engage donors by showcasing the direct impact of their contributions.

Case Study # 2

Movember Foundation - Empowering Donors through Peer-to-Peer Fundraising

The Movember Foundation, a global men's health charity, has successfully utilized peer-to-peer fundraising to engage donors and amplify their reach. They encourage individuals to grow mustaches during the month of November and seek sponsorship for their efforts. This approach not only raises funds but also creates a sense of camaraderie and empowers individuals to become advocates for men's health. Movember leverages the power of social networks to amplify their message and encourage individuals to become fundraisers themselves, expanding their donor base and impact.

Key Takeaway: Peer-to-peer fundraising can harness the power of personal networks, empower donors, and amplify the reach of fundraising efforts.

Case Study # 3

DonorsChoose - Personalized Giving for Education

DonorsChoose is an online platform that connects teachers with donors who wish to support specific classroom projects and needs. They have created a donor-centric model that allows individuals to choose the projects they want to support based on their interests and preferences. Donors can see the impact of their contributions through updates, photos, and thank-you notes from the teachers and students they have helped. This personalized approach enhances donor engagement and provides a tangible connection between donors and the outcomes of their support.

Key Takeaway: Personalized giving experiences that allow donors to support specific projects and see the impact of their contributions can foster a deeper connection and increase donor satisfaction.

Case Study # 4

St. Jude Children's Research Hospital - Long-Term Donor Relationships

St. Jude Children's Research Hospital has built a strong donor-focused fundraising program based on cultivating long-term relationships. They prioritize stewardship and engagement by regularly updating donors on the progress of their research and sharing stories of children who have benefited from their treatments. They host donor appreciation events and provide opportunities for donors to visit the hospital and meet the patients and families they support. By emphasizing the importance of donors' contributions and fostering a sense of community, St. Jude creates lasting and meaningful relationships with their supporters.

Key Takeaway: Cultivating long-term donor relationships through stewardship, engagement opportunities, and personalized communication can foster donor loyalty and commitment.

Case Study # 5

American Red Cross - Rapid Response Fundraising

The American Red Cross is known for its effective rapid response fundraising during times of natural disasters and emergencies. They have developed a strong infrastructure and a well-coordinated approach to mobilize donors quickly and efficiently in times of crisis. Their ability to communicate urgent needs, provide updates on relief efforts, and offer multiple channels for donation enables them to engage donors effectively during critical situations.

Key Takeaway: Being prepared to respond swiftly and communicate urgent needs can engage donors in times of crisis and maximize fundraising efforts.

***

Engaging in Practical Exercises to Apply Learned Concepts

Practical exercises play a vital role in the learning process, allowing individuals to apply the concepts and skills they have learned in a hands-on and interactive manner. When it comes to donor-focused fundraising, participating in practical exercises is particularly valuable, as it provides an opportunity to test strategies, refine techniques, and gain practical experience in engaging with donors. In this section, we will explore the importance of engaging in practical exercises and how they help in applying learned concepts in the context of donor-focused fundraising. Here are eight reasons why you and your team will want to participate in some practical exercises. You may discover other reasons along the way...

- Practical exercises Reinforce Learning and Retention:
Engaging in practical exercises immediately after learning a new concept or skill helps reinforce the knowledge gained. By actively applying the learned material in real or simulated scenarios, individuals solidify their understanding and increase their chances of retaining the information. Practical exercises

allow participants to put theory into practice, bridging the gap between learning and application.

- Practical exercises Build Confidence:
Practical exercises provide a safe environment for individuals to build confidence in their abilities. They offer an opportunity to practice newly acquired skills and techniques, allowing participants to become more comfortable and proficient in applying donor-focused fundraising strategies. By engaging in exercises, individuals gain experience, develop their problem-solving abilities, and enhance their overall confidence in their fundraising capabilities.

- Practical exercises help Apply Critical Thinking:
Donor-focused fundraising often requires critical thinking and decision-making skills. Practical exercises provide a platform for individuals to analyze scenarios, evaluate options, and make informed decisions based on the concepts they have learned. These exercises encourage participants to think critically about the unique needs and preferences of donors, and how to tailor their strategies accordingly. Through practical exercises, individuals develop their analytical skills, enabling them to make sound judgments in real-life fundraising situations.

- Practical exercises Enhance Creativity and Innovation:
Practical exercises foster creativity and innovation in donor-focused fundraising. They encourage participants to think outside the box, explore different approaches, and experiment with new ideas. By engaging in exercises that require brainstorming, campaign design, or problem-solving, individuals can tap into their creative potential and discover innovative ways to engage donors effectively. This creativity and innovation can lead to fresh and impactful fundraising strategies.

- Practical exercises help us Learn from Mistakes:
Practical exercises offer a low-stakes environment for individuals to make mistakes and learn from them. Failure is an essential part of the learning process, and practical exercises provide an opportunity to experiment, take risks, and identify areas for improvement. By reflecting on their experiences, participants can refine their strategies, adjust their approaches, and iterate on their fundraising techniques. Through iterative learning, individuals become more adept at engaging donors and can optimize their efforts for better results.

- Practical exercises can improve Collaboration and Peer Learning:

Practical exercises often involve group activities and collaboration, providing an opportunity for participants to learn from one another. By working together, sharing ideas, and discussing different approaches, individuals gain insights and perspectives that they may not have considered on their own. Collaborative exercises promote peer learning and encourage participants to leverage the collective knowledge and experiences of the group. This dynamic exchange of ideas fosters a rich learning environment and stimulates innovative thinking.

- Practical exercises help us Bridging Theory and Practice:
Engaging in practical exercises allows individuals to bridge the gap between theoretical knowledge and real-life application. Donor-focused fundraising involves understanding the needs and motivations of donors, crafting compelling messages, and developing effective strategies. Practical exercises offer a chance to put these concepts into action and see how they play out in practical scenarios. This application-oriented approach helps participants develop a deeper understanding of the nuances of donor engagement and fundraising.

- Practical exercises provide Feedback and Continuous Improvement:

Practical exercises provide an opportunity for feedback, both from instructors and peers. Constructive feedback helps individuals identify strengths, areas for improvement, and potential blind spots in their fundraising strategies. By incorporating feedback and continuously refining their approaches, participants can enhance their fundraising knowledge.

We've talked at length about the WHY. Let's talk about the HOW. So, what kind of exercises can you and your team do that will accomplish these benefits? Here's five -

5 Exercise to Help Your Team

Exercise # 1 - Donor Persona Creation: Encourage your fundraising team to create detailed donor personas to better understand the motivations, preferences, and needs of different types of donors. This exercise helps your team tailor their fundraising strategies and messages to resonate with specific donor segments. We have talked a little about this process previously so we won't elaborate here. But, definitely check out these other exercises -

Exercise # 2 - Impact Mapping: Impact Mapping is a strategic planning technique that helps organizations align their activities and initiatives with desired outcomes and impact. It provides a visual representation of how an organization's efforts contribute to its overall goals and objectives. Impact Mapping focuses on understanding the desired impact, identifying the necessary changes in behavior or actions, and determining the key activities required to achieve those changes.

At its core, Impact Mapping is a collaborative exercise that involves key stakeholders, including team members, donors, beneficiaries, and other relevant parties. The process begins by defining the ultimate goal or desired impact of the organization. This could be a broad outcome, such as improving education accessibility, reducing poverty rates, or increasing environmental sustainability. The goal should be meaningful, inspiring, and clearly linked to the organization's mission.

Once the goal is established, the next step is to identify the actors or beneficiaries who are expected to change their behavior or actions to contribute to the desired impact. These actors could be donors, volunteers, policymakers, or individuals from the target community. By focusing on the actors, Impact Mapping ensures that the organization's efforts are directly connected to the people who will bring about the desired change.

The next stage involves mapping out the changes in behavior or actions required from the identified actors. This step helps clarify the specific outcomes or results that need to be achieved to drive the desired impact. For example, if the goal is to improve education accessibility, the desired outcomes might include increased enrollment rates, improved learning outcomes, or enhanced teacher training. By breaking down the goal into concrete outcomes, organizations can better understand the steps required to achieve the desired impact.

Once the outcomes are defined, the Impact Map is expanded further by identifying the key activities that need to be undertaken to facilitate the desired changes. These activities can include fundraising campaigns, awareness programs, capacity-building initiatives, policy advocacy, or any other action that helps drive the identified outcomes. Each activity is linked to the specific outcome it aims to address, creating a clear cause-and-effect relationship within the Impact Map.

Throughout the Impact Mapping process, organizations should continuously assess and prioritize their activities based on their potential to contribute to the desired impact. This involves evaluating the feasibility, cost-effectiveness, and alignment with organizational resources and capabilities. By focusing resources on activities that have a higher likelihood of driving the desired outcomes, organizations can optimize their impact and maximize the effectiveness of their efforts.

The visual representation of the Impact Map serves as a communication tool that helps stakeholders understand the organization's strategy and how their contributions fit into the bigger picture. It provides a shared understanding of the organization's goals, the actors involved, the outcomes to be achieved, and the activities required. This shared understanding promotes collaboration, alignment, and accountability among team members and stakeholders.

Overall, Impact Mapping is a powerful technique for organizations to ensure that their activities are purposeful, goal-oriented, and focused on achieving meaningful impact. By mapping out the connections between desired impact, behavioral changes, and key activities, organizations can align their efforts, engage stakeholders effectively, and maximize their ability to create positive change in the world.

- Conduct a collaborative exercise where your team maps out the tangible impact of donor contributions. Create visual representations, such as flowcharts or infographics, that clearly illustrate how donations are used to make a difference. This exercise helps your team articulate the value proposition to donors and highlight the direct impact of their support.

Exercise # 3 - Storytelling Workshop: Storytelling workshopping is a collaborative exercise aimed at developing and refining compelling narratives that effectively communicate an organization's mission, impact, and goals. It involves a group of individuals coming together to explore various storytelling techniques, share personal stories, and collectively create engaging narratives that resonate with the target audience.

The first step in storytelling workshopping is to establish a clear objective. This could be to raise awareness about a specific issue, inspire action, or generate support for a cause. The objective helps guide the storytelling process and ensures that the narratives created align with the organization's goals.

Once the objective is defined, participants in the workshop are encouraged to share personal stories related to the organization's mission or the impact it has on individuals or communities. These stories can come from staff members, volunteers, beneficiaries, or other stakeholders. Sharing personal experiences adds authenticity and emotional depth to the narratives, making them more relatable and impactful.

During the workshop, storytelling techniques and principles are explored. This includes elements such as character development, conflict, resolution, and the power of emotions. Participants discuss different storytelling structures, such as the hero's journey, and how these frameworks can be applied to their narratives. They also learn about the importance of creating a strong opening, maintaining engagement throughout the story, and delivering a memorable ending.

In addition to discussing techniques, participants analyze existing stories that have effectively communicated similar messages or captured public attention. This analysis helps identify storytelling strategies that have been successful and can be adapted to the organization's context. By studying successful stories, participants gain insights into narrative structure, tone, pacing, and the use of vivid language or visual imagery.

Once participants have a deeper understanding of storytelling principles and techniques, they engage in collaborative exercises to develop and refine their narratives. This can involve small group discussions, brainstorming sessions, or individual writing exercises. Participants are encouraged to provide feedback and suggestions to help enhance each other's stories. The workshop facilitator plays a crucial role in guiding these exercises, providing constructive criticism, and fostering a supportive environment.

Throughout the workshopping process, the narratives are refined to ensure they effectively communicate the organization's message and resonate with the target audience. This may involve eliminating unnecessary details, emphasizing key points, or adding compelling anecdotes. The goal is to create narratives that are concise, impactful, and memorable.

At the end of the workshop, participants present their finalized stories to the group. This allows for further feedback and refinement, as well as the opportunity to practice delivering the stories in a confident and engaging manner. The workshop concludes with participants having a collection of compelling narratives that can be used in various communication channels, such as websites, social media, presentations, fundraising campaigns, or storytelling events.

Storytelling workshopping is an ongoing process that encourages organizations to continually refine their narratives and adapt them to different contexts or target audiences. It empowers participants to become effective storytellers and advocates for their organization's mission. By harnessing the power of storytelling, organizations can create emotional connections, engage supporters, and inspire action, ultimately amplifying their impact and advancing their cause.

- Organize a workshop where your team explores the power of storytelling in fundraising. Ask team members to share personal stories related to your organization's mission and the impact it has on individuals or communities. Discuss different storytelling techniques and identify compelling narratives that can emotionally connect with donors.

Exercise # 4 - Donor Appreciation Role Play: Donor Appreciation Role Play is a practical exercise that allows fundraising teams to practice and enhance their skills in expressing gratitude and building relationships with donors. It involves role-playing scenarios where one person assumes the role of a donor, while another person takes on the role of a fundraiser. Through these role plays, participants can gain insights into effective donor-centered communication, improve their interpersonal skills, and learn how to create meaningful connections with supporters.

The first step in Donor Appreciation Role Play is to define different scenarios that fundraisers commonly encounter when interacting with donors. These scenarios can include situations such as expressing appreciation for a recent donation, providing updates on the impact of the donor's support, or discussing future opportunities for involvement. The scenarios should be realistic and reflective of the organization's fundraising context.

Participants are then paired up, with one person assuming the role of the donor and the other as the fundraiser. They take turns enacting the scenarios, allowing each participant to experience both sides of the interaction. This approach provides valuable perspective and empathy, enabling participants to understand the donor's expectations, emotions, and motivations.

During the role play, participants should focus on developing key communication skills. This includes active listening, empathy, clear and concise messaging, and adapting to the donor's communication style. Fundraisers should strive to create a comfortable and positive environment that encourages open dialogue and engagement.

After each role play, participants should provide feedback to one another. This feedback can focus on strengths, areas for improvement, and suggestions for enhancing the interaction. Constructive criticism and guidance should be offered to help participants refine their approach and develop effective donor-centered communication skills.

The workshop facilitator plays a crucial role in guiding the role plays and providing additional insights and coaching. They can offer tips on effective communication techniques, help participants navigate challenging scenarios, and reinforce the importance of building authentic relationships with donors.

Through Donor Appreciation Role Play, participants learn how to express genuine gratitude, personalize interactions, and make donors feel valued and appreciated. They understand the significance of active listening and asking open-ended questions to better understand donor interests and motivations. Role plays also provide an opportunity to practice storytelling techniques and effectively communicate the impact of the donor's support.

In addition to improving communication skills, Donor Appreciation Role Play helps build confidence among fundraisers. By simulating real-life interactions, participants can experiment with different approaches, receive feedback, and gain confidence in engaging with donors. This increased confidence translates into more effective and meaningful donor interactions in real-world fundraising situations.

By investing time and effort into Donor Appreciation Role Play, organizations can enhance their donor-centered approach, leading to stronger relationships, increased donor retention, and potentially higher levels of giving. The exercise helps fundraisers recognize the importance of donor appreciation as a critical component of a successful fundraising strategy.

In conclusion, Donor Appreciation Role Play is a valuable exercise for fundraising teams to improve their donor-centered communication skills. It provides an opportunity to practice expressing gratitude, building relationships, and enhancing interpersonal skills. Through role plays, fundraisers gain valuable experience and feedback, enabling them to create meaningful connections with donors and ultimately strengthen the organization's fundraising efforts.

- Divide your team into pairs and assign one person as a donor and the other as a fundraiser. Conduct role play scenarios where the fundraiser interacts with the donor, expressing appreciation and providing updates on the impact of their support. This exercise helps your team practice donor-centered communication and builds skills in expressing gratitude effectively.

Exercise # 5 - Donor Journey Mapping: Donor Journey Mapping is a strategic exercise that involves visually mapping out the various touchpoints and interactions a donor has with an organization throughout their engagement. It helps nonprofits and fundraising teams gain a deeper understanding of the donor experience, identify opportunities for engagement, and optimize their fundraising efforts. By charting the donor's journey from initial contact to ongoing support, organizations can enhance personalization, build relationships, and ultimately increase donor engagement and satisfaction.

The first step in Donor Journey Mapping is to identify the key stages or milestones in a donor's journey. These stages can vary depending on the organization and the specific context, but they generally include stages such as awareness, consideration, donation, stewardship, and retention. Each stage represents a distinct phase in the donor's relationship with the organization.

Once the stages are defined, organizations examine the touchpoints or interactions that occur at each stage. These touchpoints can be both online and offline, such as website visits, social media interactions, email communications, fundraising events, phone calls, and personalized acknowledgments. Mapping out these touchpoints helps organizations visualize the donor's experience and identify the channels through which they can effectively engage and communicate.

During the mapping process, organizations also analyze the donor's emotions, motivations, and needs at each stage. This involves understanding the factors that drive a donor to engage, donate, and continue supporting the organization. By considering the donor's perspective, organizations can tailor their messaging, content, and interactions to align with the donor's expectations and enhance their experience.

Mapping the donor's journey also involves examining the gaps, pain points, or challenges that donors may encounter at each stage. This can include issues such as a lack of information, confusing donation processes, ineffective communication, or missed opportunities for engagement. Identifying these pain points helps organizations identify areas for improvement and implement strategies to address them, ultimately enhancing the donor's journey.

Once the donor journey map is complete, organizations can use it as a tool for strategic decision-making. It helps identify opportunities to deepen engagement and build relationships at each stage. For example, organizations may identify opportunities for targeted communication, personalized follow-ups, or exclusive donor events. The map also highlights areas where organizations can gather feedback, assess donor satisfaction, and continuously improve the donor experience.

Donor Journey Mapping is an ongoing process that requires regular evaluation and adjustment. As organizations gain insights from donor interactions and feedback, they can refine the donor journey map to align with changing donor preferences and expectations. By continuously evaluating the map, organizations can identify emerging trends, optimize engagement strategies, and stay responsive to donor needs.

Ultimately, Donor Journey Mapping helps organizations create a donor-centric approach, ensuring that every interaction and touchpoint is intentional and meaningful. By understanding and addressing the donor's emotions, motivations, and needs at each stage, organizations can strengthen relationships, increase donor retention, and foster long-term support. Donor Journey Mapping is a valuable tool that enables nonprofits to maximize the impact of their fundraising efforts and build sustainable donor relationships

- Collaboratively map out the donor journey from initial engagement to ongoing support. Identify touchpoints, communication channels, and opportunities for engagement at each stage. This exercise helps your team understand the donor experience and identify areas where you can enhance personalization, build relationships, and deepen donor engagement.

Chapter 8 - Developing a Donor-Centric Fundraising Plan

- **Creating a comprehensive fundraising plan centered around donor needs**
- **Setting clear goals, objectives, and key performance indicators (KPIs)**
- **Formulating a budget and timeline for fundraising activities**

Chapter 8 focuses on the crucial step of developing a donor-focused fundraising plan. A well-designed fundraising plan is essential for organizations to effectively engage donors, raise funds, and achieve their financial goals. In this chapter, we will explore the key components of a donor-focused fundraising plan and the step-by-step process to develop an effective and strategic plan.

A solid donor-focused fundraising plan provides a roadmap for organizations to identify and prioritize their fundraising objectives, strategies, and tactics. It ensures that fundraising efforts align with the needs and preferences of donors, ultimately maximizing engagement and financial support. By developing a comprehensive plan, organizations can establish clear goals, define target audiences, determine appropriate fundraising methods, and allocate resources effectively.

The first step in developing a donor-focused fundraising plan is to set clear and measurable goals and objectives. These goals should be aligned with the organization's mission and vision, taking into consideration the specific needs and priorities of donors. Whether the goal is to raise a certain amount of funds, increase donor retention rates, or expand the donor base, it is important to establish quantifiable targets that can be tracked and evaluated.

Donor research and segmentation also play a vital role in developing a donor-focused fundraising plan. Organizations must understand their donors' demographics, motivations, preferences, and giving capacity to tailor their strategies effectively. By segmenting donors into specific groups based on relevant criteria, such as giving history, engagement level, or interests, organizations can create targeted approaches and messages that resonate with each segment.

Once the donor research and segmentation are complete, organizations can determine the most effective fundraising methods and channels to reach their target donors. This may include direct mail campaigns, online fundraising, events, corporate partnerships, or major donor cultivation. The selection of methods and channels should align with the preferences and behaviors of the target donors, ensuring that fundraising efforts are engaging and accessible.

Communication will be key to donor engagement, and developing a comprehensive donor communications plan is crucial in a donor-focused fundraising strategy. The plan should outline the key messages, channels, and frequency of communication to effectively engage donors throughout their journey. Organizations should consider the use of storytelling, impact reporting, and personalized messages to build strong connections and foster donor loyalty.

Developing a donor-focused fundraising plan will require careful budgeting and resource allocation. Organizations must determine the financial resources needed to execute their fundraising strategies effectively. This includes considering expenses related to staff, marketing materials, technology, events, and donor stewardship. Allocating resources strategically ensures that fundraising efforts are well-supported and maximizes return on investment.

A donor-focused fundraising plan is a dynamic document that requires ongoing monitoring, evaluation, and adjustments. Regularly tracking the progress of fundraising activities against the set goals and objectives allows organizations to identify areas of success and areas that require improvement. By analyzing data, measuring key performance indicators, and soliciting feedback from donors and stakeholders, organizations can make informed adjustments to their strategies, optimizing their fundraising efforts for long-term success.

In summary, a successful donor-focused fundraising plan is integrated with the overall goals and strategies of the organization. It aligns with the mission, vision, and values, ensuring that fundraising efforts contribute to the organization's broader objectives. By integrating fundraising activities with other organizational initiatives, such as program development, marketing, and community engagement, organizations can leverage synergies and enhance their overall impact.

***

Creating a Comprehensive Fundraising Plan Centered Around Donor Needs

A comprehensive fundraising plan centered around donor needs is crucial for organizations to build meaningful relationships with their donors and maximize their fundraising potential. By focusing on understanding and meeting the needs of donors, organizations can create personalized and impactful fundraising strategies. In this section, we will explore the key steps involved in creating a comprehensive fundraising plan centered around donor needs.

1. Donor-Centric Approach:
To create a fundraising plan centered around donor needs, organizations must adopt a donor-centric approach. This means shifting the focus from organizational goals to understanding and fulfilling the needs, motivations, and preferences of donors. By placing donors at the center of the planning process, organizations can tailor their strategies to better engage and inspire donors to contribute to their cause.

2. Conducting Donor Research:
The foundation of a donor-centric fundraising plan lies in conducting thorough donor research. Organizations need to gather data and insights about their donors to understand

their demographics, giving patterns, communication preferences, and motivations. This can be done through surveys, interviews, donor analytics, and data analysis. The research should aim to identify common characteristics and trends among donors, enabling organizations to create targeted fundraising strategies.

3. Segmenting Donors:
Once the donor research is complete, organizations should segment their donor base into distinct groups based on shared characteristics, interests, or giving behavior. Donor segmentation allows organizations to tailor their communication and fundraising approaches to specific donor segments, increasing the relevance and effectiveness of their strategies. For example, segmenting donors based on their giving capacity can help determine appropriate ask amounts and stewardship efforts.

4. Understanding Donor Needs and Motivations:
To create a fundraising plan centered around donor needs, organizations must gain a deep understanding of the needs and motivations driving donor giving. Donors may have emotional connections to the cause, a desire for impact, or specific interests they wish to support. By uncovering these needs and motivations, organizations can design

fundraising initiatives that resonate with donors on a personal level and provide them with a sense of fulfillment and impact.

5. Setting Clear Fundraising Goals:
Once organizations have a clear understanding of donor needs and motivations, they can set specific and measurable fundraising goals. These goals should align with the organization's overall objectives while taking into account the needs and capacities of donors. For example, if a significant portion of donors express interest in supporting a specific program, the fundraising plan can include a goal for funding that program. Clear goals provide a benchmark for success and guide the implementation of fundraising strategies.

6. Crafting Donor-Centric Messages and Appeals:
Effective communication is vital in a donor-centric fundraising plan. Organizations should craft messages and appeals that speak directly to the needs and motivations of donors. This involves using language and storytelling techniques that resonate with donors and demonstrate the impact of their contributions. By highlighting the ways in which donors can make a difference and emphasizing the value of their support, organizations can inspire greater engagement and generosity.

7. Developing Donor Engagement Strategies:

Donor engagement is a key element of a comprehensive fundraising plan centered around donor needs. Organizations should develop strategies to cultivate and nurture relationships with donors. This can include personalized thank-you notes, regular updates on the impact of donations, exclusive donor events, and opportunities for involvement and feedback. Building a strong and ongoing connection with donors enhances their loyalty and encourages long-term support.

8. Implementing Multi-Channel Fundraising Approaches:
To meet the diverse needs and preferences of donors, organizations should implement multi-channel fundraising approaches. This means utilizing various communication channels, such as direct mail, email, social media, and events, to reach donors where they are most receptive. By providing multiple giving options, such as online platforms, text-to-give, or recurring donations, organizations can accommodate donors' preferences and make the giving process convenient and accessible.

***

Formulating a Budget and Timeline for Fundraising Activities

Formulating a budget and timeline is a crucial aspect of planning successful fundraising activities. A well-thought-out budget ensures that resources are allocated effectively, while a realistic timeline provides a roadmap for executing fundraising strategies in a timely manner. In this article, we will explore the key steps involved in formulating a budget and timeline for fundraising activities.

1. Assessing Fundraising Needs:
Before creating a budget and timeline, organizations should assess their fundraising needs. This involves determining the financial goals to be achieved through the fundraising activities. By understanding the specific needs and priorities, organizations can set realistic targets that align with their overall fundraising objectives.

2. Identifying Revenue Sources:
To create an accurate budget, organizations need to identify potential revenue sources. These may include individual donations, corporate sponsorships, grants, events, or other fundraising initiatives. By identifying the sources of revenue, organizations can estimate the income they expect to generate from each source and incorporate them into the budget.

3. Estimating Expenses:
Estimating expenses is a critical step in formulating a fundraising budget.

Organizations should consider both direct and indirect costs associated with their fundraising activities. Direct costs may include marketing materials, event venue rentals, catering, staff salaries, and technology expenses. Indirect costs, such as overhead expenses and administrative fees, should also be factored into the budget. Accurate estimation of expenses ensures that the fundraising activities remain financially sustainable.

4. Allocating Resources:
Based on the estimated expenses and revenue projections, organizations need to allocate resources accordingly. This involves determining the proportion of resources to be allocated to different fundraising activities. For example, if a significant portion of revenue is expected from a specific fundraising event, more resources may be allocated to its planning and execution. Effective resource allocation ensures that the budget is balanced and optimized for achieving fundraising goals.

5. Considering Contingency:
In the budgeting process, it is essential to consider contingency funds. Unexpected expenses or unforeseen circumstances may arise during fundraising activities. Allocating a portion of the budget as contingency funds provides a safety net and allows organizations to address any unforeseen challenges without compromising the overall fundraising plan.

6. Creating a Realistic Timeline:
Once the budget is formulated, organizations need to create a realistic timeline for their fundraising activities. The timeline should outline the sequence of events, deadlines, and milestones to be achieved throughout the fundraising process. Consideration should be given to factors such as donor communication schedules, event planning and promotion, grant application deadlines, and reporting requirements. A well-structured timeline ensures that fundraising activities are executed in a timely manner and maximizes the chances of success.

7. Aligning with Fundraising Seasons and Donor Behavior:
When formulating a timeline, organizations should consider fundraising seasons and donor behavior patterns. Different times of the year may be more favorable for certain fundraising activities or donation campaigns. For example, holiday seasons or special events may present opportunities for increased donor engagement. By aligning fundraising activities with the timing and preferences of donors, organizations can optimize their fundraising efforts.

8. Monitoring and Evaluation:
Once the budget and timeline are established, organizations should regularly monitor and

evaluate their progress. Monitoring allows organizations to track income and expenses, ensuring that they remain within the allocated budget. Evaluation helps identify any deviations or adjustments that need to be made to the budget or timeline. Regular review and assessment of fundraising activities enable organizations to make informed decisions and optimize their strategies for better outcomes.

9. Flexibility and Adaptability:
While it is important to have a well-defined budget and timeline, organizations should also remain flexible and adaptable. Fundraising activities may encounter unforeseen challenges or opportunities along the way. Being open to adjustments and modifications allows organizations to respond effectively to changing circumstances and make necessary course corrections.

***

Chapter 9 - What We've Learned and How to Sell It

This book has imparted valuable knowledge and skills in the field of fundraising and donor engagement. Readers should have gained a comprehensive understanding of the following key areas:

1. Fundraising Principles and Strategies: Readers have learned the fundamental principles and strategies of effective fundraising. They understand the importance of donor-centric approaches, setting clear fundraising goals, and implementing diverse fundraising methods to engage donors and raise funds.

2. Donor Research and Segmentation: Readers have learned the importance of conducting donor research and segmentation to better understand donor demographics, motivations, and preferences. They can now segment donors into distinct groups and tailor their fundraising strategies to meet the specific needs and interests of each segment.

3. Communication and Relationship Building: Readers have acquired skills in effective

communication and relationship building with donors. They have learned to craft donor-centric messages and appeals, utilize storytelling techniques, and employ various communication channels to engage and inspire donors.

4. Donor Stewardship and Engagement: Readers have learned the importance of donor stewardship and engagement to cultivate long-term relationships with donors. They have gained knowledge on developing personalized stewardship strategies, expressing gratitude, providing impact updates, and creating opportunities for donor involvement.

5. Fundraising Planning and Management: Readers have learned how to develop comprehensive fundraising plans centered around donor needs. They can set realistic fundraising goals, formulate budgets, allocate resources, create timelines, and monitor and evaluate fundraising activities to ensure successful implementation.

6. Ethical and Legal Considerations: Readers have gained an understanding of the ethical and legal considerations in fundraising. They have learned about donor privacy, data protection, transparency, and compliance with relevant laws and regulations.

7. Fundraising Trends and Innovations: Readers have been introduced to current trends and innovations in fundraising. They have explored topics such as online fundraising, crowdfunding, social media strategies, and leveraging technology to enhance fundraising efforts.

8. Team Collaboration and Peer Feedback: Readers have developed skills in team collaboration and leveraging peer feedback for continuous improvement. They understand the importance of working collaboratively, providing constructive feedback, and learning from others' experiences and perspectives.

Overall, readers should have gained a holistic understanding of donor-focused fundraising, equipping them with the knowledge and skills to develop strategic fundraising plans, engage donors effectively, and achieve their fundraising goals. They are prepared to navigate the dynamic landscape of fundraising, adapt to changing donor preferences, and make a meaningful impact in their organizations and communities.

You say, 'Wonderful, Art. Thank you for sharing so much helpful information. Now tell me how I can use it to make some money...'

The above statement isn't meant to be crass or trivial but bring all of this knowledge into perspective. Raising money for your clients isn't just for fun. Professional fundraisers also need to earn a living and build a career.

***

Here are ten ways fundraisers can sell their services and expertise -

1. Develop a strong online presence: Professionals fundraisers should invest in creating a compelling website and active social media profiles to showcase their expertise, success stories, and client testimonials. This online presence will help attract potential clients and demonstrate their value.

Share your expertise on websites such as LinkedIn, Facebook, Twitter, Instagram. Write a blog on your website. You want to be seen as someone who is active in the space, knowledgable about the subject and willing to help others.

2. Offer free educational resources: By creating and sharing valuable content such as blog posts, e-books, webinars, or podcasts related to fundraising strategies, professionals fundraisers can establish themselves as thought leaders. This positions them as trusted advisors and can lead to client inquiries.

In terms of created content, you have to 'give away' knowledge of value to others. Sometimes consultants believe they should share little scraps of information but save the 'good stuff' only for paying customers. Unfortunately, this approach won't win you any fans or clients. No, while it seems counter-intuitive to share real knowledge of value, you must share to demonstrate your expertise in the subject matter. Give away some of the 'good stuff.'

3. Attend industry conferences and events: Participating in fundraising conferences, workshops, and networking events allows professionals fundraisers to meet potential clients face-to-face. They can deliver presentations, engage in panel discussions, and connect with individuals seeking fundraising expertise.

Speaking at a conference or workshop makes you an instant 'expert.' Great, you say. But, how do I get invited to speak? Volunteer! Most of these events are looking for people to make presentations. Contact them and suggest you can present information on a topic of interest to the group. Forget about whether they will pay you or not (They probably won't; But, you'll probably get free entry into the event...). Spend some time prior to making contact brainstorming a topic that you believe this group would be interested in learning more about. Spend some additional thought on a creative title for your presentation. The title sells it.

If your title is, 'Another Boring Talk on Fundraising' you're doomed. The event organizers won't be interested and neither will your potential audience. But, if you jazz it up a bit, '10 Easy Ways to Get Money in the Mail From Your Consulting Business,' you've at least got my ear. You'd better be good and you'd better deliver on at least half of them but you'll get some interest on the part of the event or workshop proprietors. (Next, go out and research the heck out of your topic so you've got great content to deliver!)

4. Collaborate with nonprofits and organizations: By partnering with nonprofits on pro bono or discounted projects, professionals fundraisers can demonstrate their capabilities and generate word-of-mouth referrals. Collaborating with other professionals, such as grant writers or marketing consultants, can also create opportunities for cross-referrals.

We've all got to eat and pay the bills. I get it, you get it. But, too much is made of doing everything for a fee. Some of your best potential clients and business opportunities will come from volunteering your time and expertise for free. Using this strategy can put you in front of people and organizations you would probably never do business with if you were competing for a contract to work for them. Engaging with them for free let's them meet and get to know you. It allows them to see the quality of your work and the sharpness of your thinking.

Personal Timeout (PT) - Two instances come to mind where I initially engaged with organizations for free, volunteering my services just because I believed strongly in what they were doing. The act of volunteering got me involved with the first non-profit. It seems organizations, like many for-profit businesses cannot resist the offer of 'free' help. I didn't have to do that much work from a time involvement standpoint. But, soon the president of the group was suggesting that I begin to bill the organization for my services. 'They appreciated my work but did not want to take advantage of me or my expertise.' This happened organically. I did not approach the leaders and suggest they begin to pay me. They volunteered AFTER I had donated some time and talent.

The second scenario was very similar. The leader of a non-profit which I had just met at a networking event asked for my help. He had no money to pay me for help. I knew it and he knew it. I could have told him, 'I'm too busy' or 'I don't do work for free; I've got to eat just like you do.' Neither of these responses would have gotten me involved in the cause. Sure, I may have saved my time. I could have mentally been proud of myself for letting someone know, 'My services are valuable. I don't give them away for free!' But, I would have missed out on the chance to make a difference in the lives of orphan children in Asia.

This situation is ongoing. But, I have no doubt that as the financial profile of the organization is raised, these guys will become a paying client of mine. And, why wouldn't they? They know me. They trust me. I've been in the trenches with them when they needed help. Who would you trust somebody that has been in battle with you or someone you has been on the sidelines, telling you, 'Whenever you're ready to pay me, I'll throw you a lifeline!'

5. Leverage past success stories: Highlighting previous successful fundraising campaigns and showcasing the results can be an effective way to attract new clients. Professionals fundraisers should compile case studies and testimonials to demonstrate their track record and build credibility.

Part of this leveraging success stories is to gather referrals. A past boss of mine used to say, '*The best sale is a reference sell*.' And, he's right. It's certainly the easiest sale. If you work with Joe and Jane and they are happy, wouldn't it be great if they told their good friends at another organization, Sam and Samantha, 'We had a good experience working with Art. He helped us tremendously. You should consider using him for your org.' How much convincing do you think you would have to do to get Sam and Samantha to work with you? Probably not much.

I hear you thinking (metaphorically speaking) - 'Art, that's a solid idea. But, it's easier said than done. How am I going to get a bunch of references to use with other potential clients?' Answer - ASK FOR THEM! Every time you have a successful outcome, i.e., you just worked with client X and helped them raise money for next year's budget. They are happy as clams. Ask them (you already know these people. They aren't strangers you're approaching, asking for a favor...), 'Are you happy/pleased with the results of our work?' They will likely answer, 'Yes. It's been great/wonderful/the best.' Ask them right then, 'Would you be willing to write me a reference so I can show my next potential client?'

I have never had someone turn down this request. If they are happy/satisfied with your work, they will write a short reference letter. It doesn't need to be more than a paragraph. Be sure to ask them if they mind you using their reference on your social media pages. (If they say, 'No, don't use it, then don't use it.) Now, here's the caveat to this process. _Only ask those clients you know are happy with the fundraising outcome or your work._ If you suspect at all they are less than pleased with the outcome or process, don't ask them for a reference. They probably wouldn't give you one.

6. Offer personalized consultations: Providing free initial consultations or assessments can help professionals fundraisers understand the specific needs of potential clients. These consultations can be used to demonstrate your expertise, offer tailored recommendations, and present the value you can bring to the client's fundraising efforts.

One thing I have offered with some success is a free initial financial analysis. This requires some time and effort. But, they (the client) must provide their financial data. This information gives you a window into the workings of the organization and allows you to begin to formulate a strategy to engage with them. It's also very helpful to them. Part of your analysis is going to suggest what you think their financial potential could be based on _their_ data.

1st NOTE: _Go broad with any financial projections at this point._ If your projections are too specific and they fall short of what the group hopes to raise, you may lose the sale. I had this happen one time with a private school I hoped to work with... They asked me to prepare a projection on what I thought they could raise financially for a new building. I captured their financial data, crunched the numbers, did some research on other schools in the area and made my projection - $1.5M over the next three years. They had hoped for $5M and questioned me about my calculations.

Hoping to impress them with my financial acumen, I went through the details of the forecasting process. We looked at past donors, the size of their largest gifts, etc. I was sure I had 'wowed' them with my financial wizardry. Nope. They chose not to work with me. If I couldn't get them to $5M and didn't believe they could do it, why should they employ me? They used another firm and raised $1.4M. I felt vindicated. They raised what I told them they would raise. Only problem was, they were paying the *other* firm to help them raise the $1.4M, not me...

2nd NOTE: - *Don't be a 'dream killer' with your projections.* Before you deliver your forecast, try to determine what the leaders think/want/believe they can and need to raise. I don't want to tell them outright, 'There's no way you can raise that amount...!' I want to be on their side, believing we can be successful raising money. Plenty of people have already told them, 'It can't be done.' Am I suggesting you lie to the client? Raise their hopes, take the fee and then when things fall way short tell them, 'I sure hate that for you...?" No. This will only make them mad and cause them to give you a bad referral to their friends and neighbors.

So, how do we deal with this situation? I have told clients who have expressed the desire/belief they can raise more than my analysis suggests, 'I can see that number. It may take us a couple of fundraising campaigns to get there. But, I can see it...' And, that is a true statement. The $5M the school client wanted was possible; just probably not in a single capital campaign. Two or three campaigns though could have easily garnered that amount.

7. Develop strategic partnerships: By forming alliances with complementary service providers, such as event planners, public relations agencies, or donor management software companies, professionals fundraisers can expand their reach and offer comprehensive solutions. This collaboration can lead to joint marketing efforts and shared referrals.

8. Utilize email marketing campaigns: Building an email list of interested prospects and

regularly sending targeted newsletters or updates can keep professionals fundraisers top-of-mind for potential clients. These emails can include relevant fundraising tips, success stories, and information about the services they offer.

Again, they key here is to deliver great content of value in your emails. Just sending out a digital flyer of your services won't do much in the way of generating new business. But, giving potential clients real tips, advice, expertise will help them see you as the go-to person when they need your services.

9. Provide training workshops and seminars: Organizing fundraising training workshops or seminars allows professionals fundraisers to showcase their expertise while helping organizations build their fundraising skills. These events can be offered as paid services or as a way to generate leads for future consulting engagements.

Plenty of people in all sorts of industries are organizing workshops and training courses for potential clients. I've seen this in particular in the area of arts and crafts. You enjoy wood carving / knitting / sewing / painting, whatever hobby diversion. Maybe you even hope to make it a side-hustle one day. If you see a workshops that is focused on your interest that is inexpensive, say $20, chances are you'll sign-up just for the chance to learn more from an expert in the field.

Fundraisers can do the same thing. Offer a workshop about how to get or identify significant donors. What non-profit doesn't need significant donors? They are the lifeblood of most groups. Charge $49 to attend. Offer a money back guarantee. 'I will help you identify at least one significant donor that you weren't aware of or your money back.' As an attendee, what have I got to lose? As a fundraiser, what have you got to lose? You may identify several potential clients, make some new connections that will be helpful and even make a little money for the time invested... Win. win. win. win.

10. Network within professional associations: Actively participating in professional associations dedicated to fundraising or nonprofit management can help professionals fundraisers connect with potential clients. By attending events, volunteering for committees, or contributing to industry publications, they can establish relationships and establish themselves as trusted experts.

Remember that each professional fundraiser's approach may vary depending on their specific expertise, target audience, and market conditions. It's important to continuously review, refine and adapt these strategies based on feedback and results that you receive.

Chapter 10 - Now What? Consulting Scenarios and Assessments

The material that follows is from real-life situations and scenarios that non-profits and professional fund raisers have encountered. Hopefully, these exercises will expand your thinking as you determine what you might do in a similar situation.

Changing Projects / Priorities

Scenario # 1 - What would you do as a fundraiser? A non-profit is raising money for a new building but decided mid-capital campaign to switch to a different, less popular project. As details of this change began to become public knowledge, some donors were unhappy because they were personally invested in the new building project. These donors began to make their views known to other supporters in hopes of forcing the non-profit to switch back to the original project. What advice would you give to this non-profit to ensure their capital campaign doesn't collapse?

***

RECOMMENDATIONS

Switching to a different project mid-campaign can be challenging for a non-profit organization, but with the right strategies and communication, it is possible to ensure the capital campaign remains successful. Here are some pieces of advice for the non-profit to navigate this situation:

- Clear communication: Be transparent with your donors about the reason for the project switch. Clearly explain the new project's importance, impact, and alignment with the organization's mission. Assure donors that their contributions will continue to make a significant difference in the community.

- Show continuity: Highlight the connection between the initial project and the new one. Emphasize how the non-profit's overarching goals and values remain the same, even though the specific project has changed. This will help donors see the logic behind the switch and understand the organization's decision-making process.

- Reassess fundraising target: Review the financial needs for the new project and adjust the fundraising target if necessary. Make sure the target is realistic and achievable, given the new project's scope and requirements.

- Engage with major donors personally: Reach out to major donors individually to discuss the reasons for the project change and address any concerns they may have. Personalized communication can make a significant difference in maintaining their support.

- Provide options for donors: Offer donors the option to redirect their contributions (if they have already made them) to the new project or choose another initiative within the organization that resonates with their interests. Giving donors agency in their giving decisions can strengthen their commitment to the organization.

- Showcase success stories: If the non-profit has already made progress on the initial project, share success stories and outcomes achieved to date. This demonstrates the organization's ability to deliver results and builds confidence in its ability to succeed with the new project.

- Rebrand the campaign: If necessary, consider rebranding the capital campaign to reflect the new project's goals and objectives. You may need a new theme, new logo, new look. A fresh branding approach can generate renewed interest and excitement among potential donors.

- Leverage social proof: Showcase endorsements and testimonials from community leaders, experts, or beneficiaries of the non-profit's work. Social proof can validate the organization's efforts and encourage others to support the new project.

- Engage volunteers and advocates: Mobilize volunteers and advocates to spread the word about the new project through social media, community events, and word-of-mouth. Enthusiastic supporters can create a ripple effect and attract more donors to the cause.

- Provide regular updates: Keep donors informed about the progress of the new project through regular updates and reports. Demonstrating transparency and accountability will maintain donors' trust and engagement.

By following these strategies and demonstrating the organization's commitment to its mission and the community's well-being, the non-profit can work to ensure the capital campaign continues to thrive despite the project switch.

Donor Fatigue / Burnout

Scenario # 2 - What would you do as a fundraiser? A non-profit is organizing its third three-year capital campaign in 10 years. The project involves paying off a mortgage for facilities that were newly purchased at the start of the first campaign. Unfortunately, the donor pool and base hasn't increased significantly during the past campaigns. Initial surveys and focus groups indicate there is donor fatigue among the faithful. Additionally, the leader and staff are displaying signs of burnout. The organization has hired you to lead their next capital effort. What would you do to make sure their next capital campaign meets its financial goals?

***

RECOMMENDATIONS

To ensure a successful next campaign and address the issues of donor fatigue and staff burnout, the non-profit should take a very strategic and thoughtful approach. Here are some key pieces of advice for the non-profit:

- Conduct a Post-Campaign Evaluation: Before launching the next capital campaign, conduct a thorough evaluation of the previous campaigns. Identify what worked well and what didn't, and gather feedback from donors, staff and volunteers. Use this information to make informed decisions and improvements for the upcoming campaign.

- Develop a Compelling Case for Support: Create a clear and compelling case for support that communicates the non-profit's mission, impact, and the importance of the new project. Success in the long run always comes back to vision. It's what attracts and repels people. Focus on the unique aspects of the next campaign / project and explain how it aligns with the organization's long-term vision.

- Segment and Personalize Appeals: The organization will have to work harder than ever to avoid sending generic appeals to all donors. Instead, segment donors based on their interests, giving history, and engagement level. Personalize the appeals to make them more relevant and engaging to each donor segment.

- Strengthen Donor Stewardship: Focus on building stronger relationships with donors throughout the year, not just during the campaign. Regularly communicate with donors to keep them informed about the organization's activities and the impact of their contributions. Just like you're going to personalize the appeals, personalize the engagements with donors. Does this major donor prefer to meet at the coffee shop? Do it. Does the other donor want you to come by their office to talk? Do it. Does the next donor prefer dinner that includes their spouse? Do it.

- Set Realistic Fundraising Goals: Avoid setting overly ambitious fundraising targets that put excessive pressure on the organization and staff. Set realistic, achievable goals based on the non-profit's financial capacity and the project's needs.

- Prioritize Staff Well-Being: Recognize and address staff burnout by implementing policies that promote work-life balance and support staff mental health. Encourage team-building activities and celebrate successes frequently to boost staff morale.

- Diversify Fundraising Strategies: Relying solely on repeated appeals may contribute to donor fatigue. Explore diverse fundraising strategies such as events, corporate partnerships, online campaigns, and planned giving to expand the donor base. If you have never considered obtaining grants, now might be a good time to investigate the possibility.

- Build a Sense of Urgency: Create a sense of urgency around the new project by highlighting the immediate and long-term impact it will have. Emphasize why it is essential to act now and how donors can make a meaningful difference. In Hollywood screenwriting parlance this is called 'creating a time clock.' Watch your favorite film and notice that there are several 'time clocks' that ramp up the sense of drama and urgency. The hero has to deliver the money in 20 minutes of the kidnap victim will be killed. The bomb has a literal timer (built-in time clock) that will go off in five minutes if the bomb expert doesn't get here. Your urgency may involve people starving or pets dying. How many are affected per hour? Per day? Per month? Per year?

- Collaborate with Past Donors: Re-engage with donors who have supported the non-profit in previous campaigns. Show them the progress made from their previous contributions and demonstrate how their continued support is crucial for the new project. If these are significant donors your messaging should be, "We can't do it without you..." Many significant donors want to play the role of hero or game changer. They may stand back as things develop and then swoop in near the end to save the day... just when it looked like the campaign was going to be a total flop.

- Monitor and Adjust: Continuously monitor the campaign's progress and donor response. If there are signs of donor fatigue or diminishing returns, be prepared to adjust the campaign strategy in real-time to re-energize the fundraising efforts.

By adopting a more thoughtful and strategic approach, focusing on donor stewardship, and prioritizing staff well-being, a non-profit can increase the likelihood of a successful next capital campaign and revitalize donor enthusiasm for supporting its cause.

Board / Leadership Conflicts

Scenario # 3 - What would you do as a fundraiser? A non-profit has Board and leadership issues such as internal conflict and disagreement over fundraiser goals and priorities. They have just hired you to help them raise money. What would you advise the non-profit to do to have a successful next capital campaign?

***

RECOMMENDATIONS

To ensure a successful next capital campaign despite the board and leadership issues, the non-profit must address these challenges and foster a collaborative and cohesive environment. Here are some key pieces of consulting advice for the organization:

- Facilitate Open Communication: Encourage open and honest communication among board members and leadership. Create a safe space for them to express their concerns, opinions, and ideas. Address any underlying conflicts and work towards finding common ground on fundraiser goals and priorities.

- Establish Clear Fundraiser Goals: Clearly define the goals and objectives of the capital campaign. Ensure that all board members and leadership are aligned with these goals to avoid conflicting agendas.

- Collaboratively Set Priorities: Involve all stakeholders in the decision-making process when setting fundraiser priorities.

This will help gain buy-in and commitment from everyone involved.

- Appoint a Mediator: If conflicts persist, consider appointing a neutral mediator or facilitator to help resolve differences and guide discussions. This person can help steer the conversation towards productive outcomes.

- Develop a Fundraising Committee: Create a fundraising committee with representatives from the board and leadership. This committee can work together to develop the campaign strategy and ensure everyone's perspectives are considered.

- Seek External Consultation: Consider seeking advice from external fundraising consultants or experts. They can provide objective insights and strategies to overcome internal challenges and improve the capital campaign's chances of success.

- Focus on the Mission: Remind the board and leadership of the organization's mission and the impact it has on the community. Emphasize that collaboration and unity are crucial to achieving the non-profit's overarching goals.

- Provide Training and Education: Offer training and educational resources to board members and leadership on effective fundraising strategies and best practices. This can equip them with the necessary skills to navigate fundraising challenges successfully.

- Evaluate Board Composition: Assess the board's composition and consider adding members with diverse skill sets and experiences related to fundraising and development. A well-rounded board can contribute fresh ideas and perspectives.

- Set Performance Metrics: Establish clear performance metrics and milestones for the campaign. Regularly review progress and adjust the strategy as needed to stay on track.

By fostering open communication, addressing conflicts, and collaboratively setting goals, the non-profit can create a more cohesive and focused fundraising effort. When everyone is aligned with the campaign's objectives, the organization will be better positioned to achieve its fundraising goals and make a positive impact on their community.

Competition

Scenario # 4 - What would you do as a fundraiser? A non-profit has discovered increasing competition from other non-profit organizations and commercial ventures pursuing similar social causes. These appear to be diverting potential donors' attention and support. They have just hired you to help them raise money. What would you advise them to do in this situation?

***

RECOMMENDATIONS

To continue raising revenue and thrive in the face of increased competition, a non-profit must differentiate itself and actively engage donors. Here are some strategies to consider:

- Identify and Highlight Unique Selling Points: Identify what makes the non-profit stand out from its competitors. It could be the organization's unique approach, specific target audience, or innovative solutions. Highlight these differentiators in marketing materials and communication with donors.

- Focus on Impact and Results: Emphasize the tangible impact and results of the non-profit's work. Share success stories, testimonials, and data that demonstrate the organization's effectiveness in achieving its mission. Donors are more likely to support initiatives with a proven track record of success.

- Engage Donors Emotionally: Appeal to donors' emotions by sharing compelling stories and personal narratives of individuals or communities the non-profit serves. Emotional connections can create a sense of empathy and loyalty, driving continued support.

- Strengthen Donor Stewardship: Invest in building strong relationships with existing donors. Regularly communicate with them, express gratitude, and keep them informed about the organization's progress and achievements. Engaged donors are more likely to continue supporting the cause.

- Diversify Fundraising Strategies: Explore diverse fundraising methods beyond traditional appeals. Consider events, online campaigns, peer-to-peer fundraising, corporate partnerships, or cause-related marketing collaborations to reach new audiences.

- Collaborate with Partners: Form strategic partnerships with other organizations, businesses, or community groups that share similar goals. Collaborative efforts can expand the non-profit's reach and resources.

- Offer Customized Giving Opportunities: Tailor giving opportunities to suit different donor preferences and interests. Offer options for one-time donations, monthly giving, specific projects, or long-term sponsorships.

- Leverage Digital Marketing: Utilize digital platforms and social media to reach a broader audience and engage potential donors. Invest in compelling content, storytelling, and multimedia to stand out in a crowded online landscape.

- Host Engagement Events: Organize events that foster meaningful connections between donors and the organization. These could be donor appreciation events, community gatherings, or informative workshops.

- Emphasize Transparency and Accountability: Demonstrate transparency in financial reporting and use of funds. Go beyond the routine reporting. Show donors that their contributions are being utilized effectively and responsibly.

•   Continuous Innovation: Regularly assess and update fundraising strategies to adapt to changing donor preferences and market trends. Be open to new ideas and continuously seek ways to improve fundraising efforts.

•   Long-Term Donor Cultivation: Pursue a long-term donor cultivation strategy. Focus on nurturing relationships with potential donors, even if they don't contribute immediately. Consistent engagement can lead to future support.

By leveraging its unique strengths, telling compelling stories, diversifying fundraising approaches, and building strong relationships with donors, a non-profit can overcome competition and continue raising revenue to support its vital social causes.

Economic Downturn

Scenario # 5 - What would you do as a fundraiser? The Economy is going south. Inflation is raging, unemployment is rising. All of the signs that another Recession is beginning are present. Individuals and businesses have reduced disposable income and other financial constraints. A non-profit just hired you to help them raise money in tough times. What would you advise them to do?

***

RECOMMENDATIONS

During an economic downturn, non-profits may face challenges in fundraising, but there are several strategies they can adopt to navigate through this difficult period. Here are some pieces of advice for the struggling non-profit:

- Assess and Prioritize Programs: Conduct a thorough assessment of the non-profit's programs and initiatives. Identify the ones that align most closely with the organization's mission and have the highest impact. Prioritize these programs for funding and consider temporarily scaling back less critical activities.

- Communicate Impact: Clearly communicate the non-profit's impact and the value of its work to potential donors. Show how contributions directly support beneficiaries and make a positive difference in the community, which can inspire donors to continue or increase their support.

- Focus on Donor Stewardship: Strengthen relationships with existing donors by providing regular updates on the organization's activities and how their contributions are being used. Demonstrating transparency and accountability can build trust and encourage continued support.

- Diversify Revenue Streams: Explore alternative sources of revenue beyond traditional fundraising. Consider partnerships, corporate sponsorships, social enterprises, grants, or online fundraising campaigns to supplement funding.

- Adapt Fundraising Strategies: Reevaluate fundraising strategies and tactics to suit the current economic climate. Explore digital fundraising options, virtual events, and crowdfunding campaigns to reach potential donors remotely.

- Collaborate with Other Non-Profits: Seek opportunities to collaborate with other non-profits on joint initiatives or fundraising efforts. By pooling resources and expertise, organizations can have a more significant impact and reach broader audiences.

- Pursue Emergency Funding: Research and apply for emergency funding opportunities or grants specifically designed to assist non-profits during economic downturns. Government agencies, foundations, and corporations may offer financial support in times of crisis.

- Focus on Major Donors: Concentrate efforts on cultivating major donors who have the capacity to give significant contributions. Major gifts can play a crucial role in sustaining the organization during challenging economic times.

- Volunteer Engagement: Leverage the power of volunteers to support fundraising efforts and amplify the non-profit's message. Engaged volunteers can be advocates for the cause and help expand the organization's reach.

- Implement Cost-Cutting Measures: Evaluate operational expenses and implement cost-cutting measures where possible without compromising the organization's core functions. This can help stretch the available funds and demonstrate financial prudence to donors.

- Show Resilience and Flexibility: Acknowledge the economic challenges openly and demonstrate the organization's resilience and ability to adapt. Donors are more likely to support non-profits that show determination and resourcefulness in difficult times.

- Long-Term Planning: Develop a long-term financial sustainability plan that considers various economic scenarios and incorporates strategies to navigate future economic downturns effectively.

By implementing these strategies, a struggling non-profit can improve its chances of weathering the downturn and continue fulfilling its mission despite the economic financial constraints. Adaptability, strong communication, and a focus on impact will be key elements in navigating through challenging economic times.

APPENDIX A

Lance's Story

On July 23, 1970, my wife Connie gave birth to a beautiful baby boy. For three years we had tried unsuccessfully to start a family, so our joy was great with the arrival of what was to be our only biological child.

We later adopted a daughter.

Lance, the biological son was born before it became acceptable for the father to be present in the delivery room. A fact for which I have been forever grateful! I waited in the hallway just outside the delivery room. At precisely 4:13am I heard a sound I will never forget. Lance's first cry. The nurse emerged with a smile to say, "You have a baby boy." I responded, "Yes, I know, I never doubted that I would have a son."

I could hardly wait to get Connie and Lance out of the hospital and back home so I could get my hands on him. The wonderful glow of fatherhood was soon dimmed however when I was asked to visit the business office of the hospital.

They wanted me to pay for Lance. In fact, it seemed to me that my wife and child might be held hostage till the hospital bill was settled. I wrote the check paying all the expenses in full, freed my family and we made our escape.

Art Fuller, PhD   190

That check turned out to be only one of the first of hundreds maybe thousands I would write on Lance's behalf.

Children are expensive. There was formula to buy. Food to buy. Doctors visits. Vaccinations...assaulted my bank account...diapers and toys took their toll. And clothes were a constant drain. Just about the time we built a great wardrobe for the kid he would grow, forcing us to start all over again... As his age and size increased, so did the expense as soon it was baseball gloves, Nike shoes and uniforms...there were glasses for his eyes and braces for his teeth. And then disaster struck. Lance became a teenager. Now it was cars and dates and name-brand clothes.

Then came college. Lance had always and only wanted to be an architect. It seemed he would be in school until he was forty years old. Expenses soared. Tuition, books, drawing tools. But of course, just like parents everywhere, were happy to help him. And we did all we could to support his growth and his dream.

And then one day, Lance died. On Halloween day 1991, we buried 21 year old Lance in our church's country cemetery.

That afternoon we walked away from his grave and since that day we have never spent another nickel on Lance.

That's how I learned that death is cheap.

Death can be sustained without expense.

It is living that is costly. It is growth that is expensive.

Our dreams, visions, and hopes require sacrifice.

That's why I will always belong to a church that needs money. A living, growing, thriving church will always require the continual, consistent, and conscientious *financial support of its members.*

POSTSCRIPT

I wrote this book / manual in part because I wanted an easy reference guide that I could pick up and topically find help. While I authored the material, even my feeble memory can't recall everything all the time. I also knew that taking a donor-centric, donor-focused approach is the correct way to raise finances and build relationship. It's about *them*, the donors, not us, the fundraisers or organizations.

My hope is that you will keep this tome handy. When you encounter a situation that warrants some guidance, I trust you will reach for it and find the information you need, quickly and easily.

From my perspective, professional fundraisers should be proud of several aspects of their work and the impact they have on their organizations and communities. Fundraisers can take pride in the fact they are making a Difference. Fundraisers play a vital role in securing the financial resources that enable non-profit organizations to make a positive impact on society. They can take pride in knowing that their efforts directly contribute to social causes and bring about positive change. Fundraisers build and nurture relationships with donors, volunteers, and other stakeholders that are essential for the long-term sustainability and success of the organization, and fundraisers can be proud of the connections they create.

In short, professional fundraisers play a critical role in advancing philanthropy and driving positive change. They should take pride in their ability to connect donors with causes, build meaningful relationships, and support organizations in making a lasting impact on the world. If you are counted among their number, hats off to you!

THIS PAGE LEFT INTENTIONALLY BLANK.